Thomas Mann: *Letters to Paul Amann*

THOMAS MANN

Letters to Paul Amann

◾[1915–1952]◾

Edited by

HERBERT WEGENER

Translated from the German by

RICHARD AND CLARA WINSTON

WESLEYAN UNIVERSITY PRESS

Middletown, Connecticut

Published in German as *Veröffentlichungen der Stadtbibliothek Lübeck*, Neue Reihe, Band 3, 1959

Library of Congress Catalog Card Number: 60–7258

Manufactured in the United States of America

First edition

Contents

Thomas Mann: *Letters to Paul Amann*

Introduction

THE FORTY-EIGHT letters and postcards of Thomas Mann printed here were purchased by the Municipal Library of Lübeck from the addressee, Paul Amann, the Austrian philologist and cultural historian who emigrated to the United States after the "Anschluss" of Austria. Thus a collection of letters of substantial size and importance, extending in time more than a generation and in space from the Old to the New World, came to rest in the library of the great writer's natal city. Afterward the Library was able to supplement this collection with a number of carbon copies and a draft letter of the addressee's in his own handwriting.

The letters were acquired in several stages. The bulk of them were purchased toward the end of 1955 with financial aid from the Possehl Foundation of Lübeck, whose assistance to the Library must be gratefully acknowledged once again, as so often in the past. The first group, Numbers 1–37 in this edition, date from before Thomas Mann's move to the United States. When Professor Amann left Austria in February, 1939, he feared that these letters might be confiscated at the

3

border, and therefore left them behind in the care of his friend Dr. Otto Brechler, Director of the Manuscript Department of the Vienna National Library. Here the letters survived a good many of the perils of war— *habent sua fata et litterae,* as Amann whimsically remarked: bomb damage to Dr. Brechler's house on Maxingstrasse, near Schönbrunn; a hurried change of residence; pillaging of the house by the Russians. After the war the letters could not be located for some time. They were eventually found, however, and restored to Amann by the widow of Dr. Brechler after the death of the latter in 1951.

The later purchases, made in the course of three separate transactions during 1956 and 1957, brought to the Library the letters and postcards of Mann's American period, printed here as Numbers 38–48; also fourteen copies of Amann's letters to Thomas Mann from the same period. This group of letters was bought out of the Municipal Library's acquisition fund.

We owe a debt of gratitude to Paul Amann as well as to the Possehl Foundation. To our profound sorrow, this debt can be paid here only to his memory. We must thank him for having offered these letters, accumulated over years and brought safely through so many vicissitudes, to the Municipal Library of Lübeck, and for having let them go at prices within the Library's means— which, as we know, were considerably below his original estimate. We wish also to thank the book dealer, Kurt L. Schwarz of Beverly Hills, California, who first suggested to Amann the sale of the letters.

Introduction

THE LETTERS fall naturally into three main categories, according to the time of writing:

I. Nos. 1–30, twenty-six letters and four postcards dating from 1915 to 1918, dated mostly from Munich, in eight cases from Bad Tölz, Thomas Mann's summer home in those days. It appears from the postcards and from some few preserved envelopes that these were directed in some cases to Amann's home in Vienna, in some cases to his military address (garrison station or Austrian Army postal number). These letters differ from the later ones by their length—many consist of as many as ten handwritten pages. Amann's undated holograph draft of a letter was one which he gave to the Library in conjunction with the first sale of Thomas Mann letters. The draft, obviously a reply to Thomas Mann's Letter No. 1 and therefore written in February or March of 1915, is printed in this edition as an appendix to the Thomas Mann letters.

II. Nos. 31–37, seven letters written during the years 1933–1937, all dated from Küsnacht bei Zürich and with one exception directed to Amann's home in Vienna. The last two of these letters were typewritten. The rest, like those of Group I, are written in the extremely idiosyncratic "German" script of Thomas Mann's European period, a script in which peaks and long lines are strongly emphasized and separate words, especially the short ones, tend to slant sharply downward.

III. Nos. 38–48, eight letters and three postcards dating from 1948 to 1952. All of these—with the exception of the last, a postcard from Switzerland—were written in the United States, for the most part in Pacific Palisades, California, and sent to various American addresses of Amann's, mainly Plattsburgh, New York. An earlier letter of the American period (dated December 11, 1945) remains unprinted at the request of Frau Katja Mann. These letters display the smoother, more legible "Latin" handwriting of Mann's later period, a handwriting also in evidence in the autograph corrections on the typewritten letter of September 13, 1937 (No. 37). Two of the postcards (Nos. 41 and 42, 1950 and 1951) show photographs of Thomas Mann's home in California: a part of his garden and a corner of his study, with the desk. The carbon copies of Amann's letters belonging to the same period, 1948–1955, have not been printed in the present edition.

It is obvious from the above listing that there are gaps in the correspondence, amounting altogether to more than two decades. The question naturally arises, therefore, whether the Municipal Library's collection is complete, and if not, how many letters are missing. This question need be discussed only in connection with Thomas Mann's letters to Amann, since aside from the American period we possess scarcely anything of Amann's share in the correspondence.

The larger of the two gaps (1919–1934) is not due to any loss of letters, but to an actual lapsing of the correspondence. This is evident from Letter 31, and the fact has been expressly confirmed by Amann. Subsequently, the relations and the correspondence between Mann and Amann were resumed. The reasons for these events will be discussed below.

6

In the second gap (1938–1944) we know definitely of one lost letter. Amann, as he informed us on January 22, 1957, possessed the envelope of this letter, postmarked at Los Angeles May 16, 1942. The letter probably contained, Amann wrote, a recommendation from Thomas Mann to aid him in his "job-hunting at colleges." The other losses are accounted for by Amann's wanderings as a refugee. He did not arrive in the United States until several years after his departure from Vienna, and then was some time establishing himself on a firm footing in the New World.

The other missing letters concerning which we have definite information belong to years for which we possess other letters. Thus it is evident from remarks of Thomas Mann in Numbers 7, 25, and 29 that two letters and a postcard are missing from the years 1915–1918. Finally, there is missing a letter of "delightful praise" of Amann's *Tradition und Weltkrise*. Amann, as he informed us on February 12, 1956, probably gave this letter to a Viennese friend along with a copy of the book, which was published in 1934.

So MUCH FOR our acquisition of the collection of letters, and their relative completeness. In order to discuss the internal history of this correspondence we must deal at some length with the personality of Paul Amann, the circumstances of his life, and his literary and scholarly activities. Our sources are brief notices in the 1930, 1932, 1949, and 1952 editions of Kürschner's *Literatur-Kalender*, occasional passages in Amann's own writings, the letters and carbon copies of the two correspondents, and last but not least, personal information offered us by Amann in the course of our own correspondence with him during the years in which purchase of the letters was under discussion. Our account was somewhat incomplete, and because of Amann's unexpected decease it was unfortunately no longer possible to submit it to him for additions and corrections. We are therefore all the more grateful to Frau Dora Amann, who after her husband's death responded to our request for information by drawing up a careful and detailed survey of her husband's life.

Paul Amann was born in Prague on March 6, 1884, and remained in that city until his fourteenth year.[1] His further youth was spent in the German-Czech atmosphere of Saaz. He was of Jewish-German origin, but displayed an unusual receptivity to his Slavic surroundings. Thus, as he informs us in *Tradition und Weltkrise*,[2] he could always manage the rolled sibilants of Czech, which Germans find unpronounceable. However, he never really had a command of the Czech language. Amann studied German and Romance philology in Vienna and Prague. He took his doctorate at Prague with a dissertation entitled *Leopold Komperts literarische Anfänge* ["The Early Works of Leopold Kompert"] published in 1907 as Number 5 in the series *Prager Deutsche Studien* [Prague German Studies]. After teaching briefly at Reichenberg and Prossnitz, he transferred to Vienna as professor at a *Realschule*. During World War I he served at various fronts as a second lieutenant and lieutenant in the reserve, and was several times wounded. In February, 1939, he left Vienna to escape the mounting persecution and went to France, where he lived as a "beggarly refugee," first in Paris and after the fall of France in Montpellier, in the unoccupied part of France. He reached the United States in September, 1941, and for years had a hard struggle until in 1945 he obtained a post at Mohawk College, Utica, New York, which had been newly set up to meet swelling college enrollments resulting from the influx of war veterans. In 1948 he transferred to Champlain College at Plattsburgh, New York. Since he reached retirement age shortly afterward, he continued to be troubled by the problem of earning a livelihood, and this problem was eased only after the Austrian Government granted him a pension. Amann spent his last years in Fairfield, Connecticut. He died on February 24, 1958.

Amann's mind was distinguished by the variety of its interests. He possessed extensive knowledge that went far beyond the limits of his special field of language and literature. His was a restless and probing spirit, ever active and ever searching. His origins appear to have been of decisive import for the development of his thought, what he himself has called the "equivocal position of the Jew permeated with German culture" who in old Austria-Hungary had experienced "national mutations and permutations." [3] This position may explain in part his insight into and grasp of the peculiar spirit of foreign nationalities. This talent was of utmost value to him in his sustained "efforts to achieve an illumination of the underlying ideas of the German and French nature." And certainly this talent had much to do with his becoming a stimulating letter-writer.

Amann had literary ambitions, but evidently encountered difficulties in winning a place for himself. At any rate, the letters of the European period speak often of efforts Thomas Mann was making to further the publication of works by Amann. Of Amann's published scholarly writings, only the most important can be mentioned here. There are a number of literary essays, including *Theodor Fontane und sein französisches Erbe* ["Theodor Fontane's French Heritage"], published in *Euphorion*, 1914; *Goethe und das Rokoko,* published in Supplement 14 to *Euphorion,* 1921; *Plûtot une injustice qu'un désorde*—an episode of the campaign in France, published in the *Jahrbuch der Sammlung Kippenberg,* 1931; in addition, two papers on Thomas Mann, which we shall discuss in another context. There is also a historical essay, *Napoleons Dynamik* ["Napoleon's Dynamism"] which appeared in the *Insel-Almanach* for 1923; this was preceded by a selection of Napoleon's letters and conversations published by Insel Verlag in 1921. Early in the twenties Dr. Amann likewise wrote a group of rather short essays on the cultural and social position of the Jews in various European countries. His principal work, a humanistic study of intellectual history, is *Tradition und Weltkrise.* This was published in Berlin by Schocken Verlag in 1934; unfortunately its one edition was seized by the German authorities the following year.

Since this book is frequently mentioned in the letters of the nineteen-thirties, and occasionally afterward, we shall attempt here to suggest its general character. Amann examines the deeper characteristics of the cultures and civilizations of the Far East, India, the Near

East, North Africa, and southern and western Europe, and contrasts these with the cultural forms of northern Europe. He argues that two human traditions have persisted side by side, one extremely ancient and one of comparatively recent origin. He traces these disparate traditions, whose effects continue down to the present, to a geological phenomenon: the diluvial glaciation of only one part of Europe. This hypothesis is scarcely susceptible of proof, but it has proved extremely fruitful as a device for laying bare affinities and antinomies in the history of civilizations.[4]

Amann was likewise extraordinarily productive—and from a purely commercial point of view apparently far more successful—as a translator, primarily from the French. The recent bibliography of German translations from the French edited by Hans Fromm lists more than twenty-five major translations by Amann between 1921 and 1948. Among these were books by L. C. Baudouin, J. R. Bloch, E. Coué, Maurice Maeterlinck, M. L. Martin, Guy de Maupassant, Henri de Montherlant, and Romain Rolland. The numerous translations of works by Rolland merit special attention, since Amann himself regarded them as his principal achievement, along with *Tradition und Weltkrise*. For many years a close friendship existed between Amann and Romain Rolland, founded upon the deep affection and respect the younger man felt for the older writer.[5] This relationship was to play an important role in the early period of Amann's correspondence with Thomas Mann; it brought about the beginning of the correspondence and the subsequent breaking off of it.

Amann was one of the earlier admirers of Thomas Mann. Late in life, while reading *Tonio Kröger* with a class of American veterans, he recalled the "blue-green issues of the *Neue Deutsche Rundschau*" in which he had first read the story, and could almost see its very appearance on the page.[6] In keeping with his orientation, he attempted to win a place for the German writer in the minds and hearts of Frenchmen; in March, 1912, he wrote an article in French on Emil Strauss and Thomas Mann. On the instigation of one of Romain Rolland's friends, this article was published in the weekly *L'Effort libre,* edited by J. R. Bloch. It speaks for Amann's personal integrity that he did not make use of this article to get in touch personally with Thomas Mann, whom he had not yet met at the time of its publication. In fact, the first mention of Amann's essay occurs in Letter 6. First contact between the two men arose from a more compelling circumstance: the political and philosophical antagonisms which came to the fore at the beginning of World War I.

It is well known that Thomas Mann, like other artists, writers, and scholars of the period, was aroused at the outset of the war by the unexpected violence of the Allied propaganda directed against Germany. He abandoned fiction and devoted his pen to "serving the day and the hour"—to writing in defense of Germany, her conduct of the war and her policies, her character and her culture. The fruits of this labor were a series of essays in *Die Neue Rundschau: Gedanken im Kriege* ["Thoughts in War"]; *Brief an die Zeitung Svenska Dagbladet, Stockholm* ["Letter to the Stockholm Newspaper *Svenska Dagbladet*"]; and a historical study based upon a poetic idea, *Frederick and the Great Coalition,* which endeavored to defend Germany's policies at the outbreak of the war by means of a historical parallel. After these essays, which were completed by the summer of 1915, Thomas Mann still held back from the writing of fiction. During years of painful work he continued the confrontation with history which he had begun in 1914. He plunged into an examination of fundamental questions of the times. He also broadened his frontal attack, directing his polemics not only against the external foe, but also against the pro-Allied forces within Germany, the German "civilization literari." This second phase of Thomas Mann's wartime writings was at first intended as another series of essays, and several portions were published after 1916 in various issues of *Die Neue Rundschau.* In final form the various essays appeared as a ponderous, many-layered, deep, and complex volume, the *Betrachtungen eines Unpolitischen* [*Reflections of a Non-Political Man*]. Perhaps this book may best be described in Thomas Mann's own words as a "reconnaissance in polemical form of the realm of conservative nationalism," a "Quixotic defense of nationalism and Germany's war," and a "last great rear-guard action of the romantic middle-class mentality in the face of advancing 'modernity,' an action conducted not without gallantry." [7]

The first section of our correspondence coincides with this particular phase of Thomas Mann's literary activity. The correspondence was initiated by Amann, who (as he informed us in a letter of February 12, 1956) had at that time returned from Galicia and was lying in a Vienna military hospital, recovering from a battle injury. Catching up on neglected periodical reading, he came across Thomas Mann's article in the *Rundschau* for November, 1914, the *Gedanken im Kriege.* "I felt impelled to disagree, and felt justified by my situation as a 'victim.' That is how it began."

As we have already mentioned, we possess only one of Amann's numerous letters of the period: the draft of the letter reprinted here in the Appendix. However, we can supplement our knowledge from Thomas Mann's replies in his letters, and from several hints in Amann's essay *Politik und Moral in Thomas Manns "Betrachtungen eines Unpolitischen"* ["Politics and Morality in Thomas Mann's *Reflections of a Non-Political Man*"], which appeared in 1919. It is clear that in discussing the questions of the day raised in Thomas Mann's wartime essays, Amann often took a position opposed to the views then held by Thomas Mann. For example, Amann refused to attribute the anti-German attitude of world public opinion solely to ill will and ignorance on the part of Germany's opponents. He branded Germany as reactionary and questioned her capacity for producing anything new and idealistic. On the other hand he expressed admiration for Western ideas, especially for the principles of the French Revolution. The future belonged to these, he declared. He also took issue with the intellectual currents of Thomas Mann's *Betrachtungen,* which he knew from sections printed in *Die Neue Rundschau* and from the author's letters. Amann early expressed his doubts about these ideas, and in his essay went so far as to call his criticisms "warnings." [8] Specifically, he objected to Thomas Mann's assertion that the particular quality of the German middle-class mentality was incompatible with radical politics. This argument, one of the major theses of the Mann work, will engage us again in another connection.

Amann's attitude was certainly not the product of an insurmountable hostility toward the German Reich. It derived rather from a somewhat exaggerated sense of justice [9] and from his deep sympathy with French culture and the democratic ways of life in France. In any case, Amann's presentation of this point of view seems to have acted as a powerful stimulus upon Thomas Mann. That is evident from a number of direct remarks in the letters as well as from the considerable length of some of these letters. In several cases Thomas Mann admitted that Amann was right, but Mann was obviously stimulated—perhaps most strongly—where he rejected Amann's ideas and felt it necessary to refute them. A characteristic example of this is the passage in Letter 5 in which Thomas Mann expresses his astonishment at the "honest" (by which he means "patriotic") disagreement that is aroused in him at second and third reading of Amann's "clever, at once keen and deeply considered remarks" about Germany's role in the war, and suddenly bursts out with an exclamation which anticipates one of the two mottoes of the *Betrachtungen:* "How do I come to . . ." etc.

HERE is the place for us to point out the close tie between Thomas Mann's correspondence with Amann and

Mann's literary activity during the First World War. For we find numerous ideas from the literary works, especially from the *Betrachtungen,* in these letters. In a number of cases the very same phraseology is employed. The Notes call attention to passages of this sort—without pretending to any completeness. Our aim here is to establish the time interval between the occurrence of certain passages in letters and the corresponding passages in articles or books. Several such twin passages are useless for our purposes, either because there is no way of dating with any precision the literary use of the idea, or because it seems to have been simultaneous with the letter. There are, however, a number of cases in which an idea or phrase seems clearly to have made its prior appearance in a letter, before being given its final shaping in an article or book. This is true for the earliest stages of the correspondence: the passages on the anti-German propaganda campaign in Letters 1 and 2 of February and March, 1915, anticipate passages in later writings. Similarly, we will find the passages on the nature of the Prusso-German power principle repeated almost word for word in Thomas Mann's second *Rundschau* article, the "Letter to the Stockholm Newspaper *Svenska Dagbladet.*" The author tells us, in certain prefatory remarks to the book edition of his essay on Frederick the Great, that this article was written in April, 1915. Or, to choose an example from the period during which Mann was working on the *Betrachtungen,* there is the discussion of the prospects for a reconciled and refined postwar Europe set forth in Letter 9 of February, 1916. A similar analysis, although at greater length, may be found in the *Betrachtungen,* pp. 497 ff. Here again we find numerous recapitulations of the passage in the letter, and a reference to "dreams dreamed on a pre-autumnal morn in 1917." In view of such parallels it appears quite possible that such passages were originally conceived by Thomas Mann while he was engaged in this correspondence and thus were partly inspired by the debate with Amann. This question, of course, cannot be completely resolved until a more substantial proportion of Thomas Mann's correspondence of that period is available.

We find ourselves on firmer ground wherever there is explicit reference to Amann in the *Betrachtungen,* or where he is quoted. Not that his name is actually mentioned—to our knowledge Amann's name nowhere occurs in Thomas Mann's printed writings. But that certain controversial points originated with him we know from Amann's own polemical essay of 1919, *Politik und Moral in Thomas Manns "Betrachtungen eines Unpolitischen."* In this article [10] Amann cites six instances of this type. These deserve detailed consideration, although Amann's contributions are to be found not so much in his letters as in an unprinted study of Rolland which Amann had submitted to Thomas Mann in the hope that Mann would help find a publisher for it. As is clear from Letter 9 (1916), Thomas Mann was profoundly impressed by this study.

The allusions to Amann in the *Betrachtungen* are to be found, all but one, in the first half of the chapter "Gegen Recht und Wahrheit" ["Against Justice and Truth"], pages 121–164, in which Mann takes issue with Romain Rolland. Amann is the letter-writer who is quoted on page 136, lines 4 ff. The passage in question takes exception to Thomas Mann's first essay on the war, the one which appeared in the November, 1914, issue of the *Neue Rundschau*. It does not, however—as Amann alleged in his polemical article [11]—come from his first letter to Thomas Mann, but from his second. In the same article Amann stated categorically that the rather precious expression "neurological tract" was alien to his "habit of using simple language," and that he therefore could not have used it. Here, however, his memory again played him false, as is evident from the draft of his second letter printed in the Appendix to this book.

The next passage follows immediately on page 138. Here Amann is spoken of, for he is the "Austrian mutual friend" of Thomas Mann and Romain Rolland. The key quotation on which the argument revolves—"our true books are our cathedrals"—is taken from a letter which the French writer sent to Amann on January 1, 1912, and which Thomas Mann found in Amann's study of Rolland.

Mann likewise drew upon the essay for the "truly humane and surely immortal" passage from *Jean-Christophe* ("Each of our thoughts is only a moment of our lives," etc.) which is also cited in Letter 9. Amann explains that he took the quotation not from the German edition of *Jean-Christophe* but from a prepublication printing in a French journal. It figures in the same Rolland study, and it was there that Thomas Mann found it.

The next passage (page 152) concerns Amann as the author of the above-mentioned French study of Emil Strauss and Thomas Mann which appeared in the magazine *Effort libre* in 1912. From this essay Mann cites the sentences: *"Car il [Thomas Mann] es plus Allemand et moins Latin que vous ne pourriez le croire de premier abord. C'est la son originalité."* * (*Ibid.,* page 532.)

Finally, Thomas Mann's assertion on page 154 that Rolland, in spite of his philanthropic and pacifist views, "privately" came forward in defense of the introduction of the three-year term of military service in France in 1913 is based upon Amann's study of Rolland and upon a letter of Rolland's to Amann dated July 3, 1913, in which Rolland sets down the reasons for that crucial measure, which France felt obliged to take. Rolland did, however, add a comment not quoted by Thomas Mann: that he personally disagreed with this action.

The sixth passage is to be found in an earlier section of the *Betrachtungen,* the chapter entitled "Bürgerlichkeit" ["Middle-class Mentality"]. We have already alluded to the subject, the assertion by Thomas Mann that the German middle-class mentality is incompatible with radical politics, and have seen that Amann took issue with this idea in a letter as early as 1916. Thomas Mann reviewed Amann's arguments, especially his allusions to the political activities of the Grimm brothers as members of the group known as the "Göttingen Seven," and to Uhland, Storm, and Gottfried Keller, and countered them with his own answers to Amann.[12] It may well be that the sentences enclosed in quotation marks on pages 84–85 of the *Betrachtungen* were taken word for word from a letter of Amann's now lost.

* For he is more of a German and less of a Latin than you would imagine at first glance. That is his originality.

The first segment of the correspondence between Thomas Mann and Amann ended in the summer of 1918, shortly before the publication of *Betrachtungen eines Unpolitischen,* to the substance of which Amann had made, as it were, important contributions. A copy of the book reached him before the end of the war in his garrison station at Szolnok in Hungary. He does not appear to have written any letter to the author about it. Instead, in February and March, 1919, there appeared in the newly founded magazine of arts and letters *Münchener Blätter für Dichtung und Graphik* the essay to which we have already referred several times: *Politik und Moral in Thomas Manns "Betrachtungen eines Unpolitischen."* Here Amann criticized Thomas Mann sharply and aggressively. It was this essay which led to a break in relations and in the correspondence, a break which was to last for fifteen years. The break was inevitable in view of Thomas Mann's attacks upon Romain Rolland in the *Betrachtungen.*

The public controversy between Thomas Mann and Romain Rolland began with a brief deprecating remark by Mann in his *Gedanken im Kriege* and a more massive retort by Rolland in the *Journal de Genève;* details may be found in Note 13 to Letter 1 and Note 3 to Letter 16. From the very first the personality of Romain Rolland played a significant role in the letters between Amann and Thomas Mann. Rolland was in Switzerland at the time, issuing letters and manifestoes written in a humanitarian and pacifistic spirit, in which he endeavored to bring about a reconciliation among the embattled nations. Amann attempted to defend his French friend against the charge of nationalistic partisanship and to demonstrate the purity of his motives. Presumably Amann hoped also to inculcate in Thomas Mann some of his own admiration and respect for Rolland. In this effort, however, he plainly failed. He could at any rate claim [13] that he had helped to broaden and deepen the conception of Rolland which Thomas Mann had held in 1914. This change in Mann's point of view emerges even in the polemical remarks in the *Betrachtungen*.

The sixth chapter of the *Betrachtungen* consists of a full-scale reckoning with Rolland and can scarcely have come as a surprise to Amann. Thomas Mann had already indicated in a letter of 1916 that he had by no means forgotten the French writer's attacks upon him, and that he was working on a respectful but firm rebuttal which he intended to publish in his forthcoming book.[14] As it turned out, the form and content of this retort evoked from Amann a somewhat intemperate bitterness, and he poured out his wrath against the *Betrachtungen* as a whole in his article of 1919 on that book. We shall not here look into all the reasons for the intensity of his response. Possibly the mood of those days of collapse and revolution had much to do with it, as Amann wrote to us on February 12, 1956. Thomas Mann himself understood and acknowledged [15] that Amann's bitterness stemmed from his affection and reverence for Romain Rolland. This is also not the place to consider the content of Amann's criticism. It is, however, significant that even in so sharp an essay he speaks with gratitude of the letters from Thomas Mann which had given him "so many a day of intellectual exaltation at the front, on a bed of pain, in the dreary hinterland." [16] Through all the acrimony of disputation his old love and admiration for Thomas Mann's creative work is clearly recognizable.

OUR DISCUSSION of the first period of the correspondence has been concerned chiefly with the relations of Thomas Mann to Amann. We wish now to add a few remarks of a more general nature on the importance of the letters as source material.

First and foremost, the letters are a valuable source for any study of the *Betrachtungen*. They throw light upon many details of the origin of that work. They plainly reveal the close connection in time and subject between this book and Thomas Mann's essays at the beginning of the war. Evidently the book grew directly out of these, represented an expanded continuation of them in a vein of personal confession. This is not to repudiate the influence upon the final form of the *Betrachtungen* of Heinrich Mann's famous essay on Zola, with its attacks upon his brother. But the letters do serve to corroborate the testimony of Ernst Bertram, to whom Thomas Mann confided his "endless political-antipolitical speculations." [17] As early as 1919 Bertram wrote: [18] "Historical justice demands the somewhat pedantic marginal comment that this personal conflict, central as it is to the book, was by no means its starting point. The work was begun, and large parts of it were already in existence in first draft, when Heinrich Mann's major Zola essay in the *Weisse Blätter* came to Thomas Mann's attention in 1915."

Similarly, the letters not only confirm but in many cases bring vividly to life later remarks of Thomas Mann himself. We find sentences in the letters which perfectly coincide with his subsequent account of certain events. Thus in his *Lebensabriss* ("Sketch of my Life"), written in 1930,[19] he stresses the despondency and pessimism which made his weary labors on the *Betrachtungen* a terrible trial, an intellectual torture devouring years of his life. These feelings are voiced in numerous passages in letters from the beginning of 1916 on, though we may also find the contrary remark that it has done him good to speak out at last, to say all the things which have burdened him for so long.[20] Of interest and importance is Mann's perception that by then (1916) the intellectual ambience of the work in progress had already become subjectively inadmissible.[21] It was again the influence of Amann's Rolland manuscript that led him to this admission.

We must cite another example of a later statement by Thomas Mann which is foreshadowed in the World War letters. This time it is a rather surprising one. In the *Lebensabriss* of 1930, and later also, Mann attempted to relate his painful labors on the *Betrachtungen* to *The Magic Mountain,* which he had already begun but had laid aside in favor of the essays. The *Betrachtungen,* he declared, served to "considerably lighten" the novel, which otherwise would have been burdened by far too much analytic and polemic matter. At first glance such an assertion appears to be a justification in hindsight. But in fact we find Thomas Mann making the same point clearly and directly in a letter of 1917, that is to say, seven years before the publication of the novel.[22]

The initial theme of the correspondence was, as we

have noted, political and ideological. Soon, however, a literary element entered, and was thereafter interwoven with the first subject. This, incidentally, was a typical process for Thomas Mann. According to his own testimony in later life, it was an old habit of his to consider political matters alongside of belles-lettres, and to shift back and forth between these realms.[23] The correspondence naturally turned upon Thomas Mann's own novels and shorter pieces. Thomas Mann greatly valued Amann's sensitive and accurate judgments on these earlier works of fiction, and himself spoke of *The Magic Mountain,* which he had begun shortly before the outbreak of the war and whose title he mentioned as early as 1915. A good many of his comments found their way—as was the case with the political and ideological matters—into the *Betrachtungen;* some of them cropped up later in the *Lebensabriss* of 1930 and in the "Introduction to *The Magic Mountain* for Students of Princeton University" (1939). For details we again refer to the notes.

It would be too great an enterprise to examine the correspondence in close detail and pick out all the new notes in which the letters abound. The letter form lends a vividness and directness to Mann's rebuttals of misunderstandings or injustices in contemporary criticism, or to his remarks on auguries of the coming war in his last prewar writings and on the interruption of his creative activity caused by the outbreak of the conflict.

So much for the letters of the First World War period. The later letters call for less analysis, since at the time of their writing Amann's personality was of far less importance to Thomas Mann. Consequently, the letters of this period are shorter and far less interesting than those of the first period.

Amann resumed the correspondence in 1935, just as he had begun it in 1915. His letter addressed to Thomas Mann from Athens was received in friendly fashion. Indeed, Thomas Mann responded to this "benign resumption of relations" with surprising cordiality. He emphasized in his reply that he had never held a grudge against Amann, but also showed that he had by no means forgotten the strong attack Amann had made upon him at the end of the war.[24] The note of coolness and reserve crops up occasionally in further letters. The time was past for the forthright discussion in which the two had engaged in earlier years. Amann was to find Thomas Mann a man completely changed in many respects. Thomas Mann was no longer wrestling with his political and ideological principles. He had long since swung over to unconditional affirmation of liberalism and parliamentary democracy, to thoroughgoing opposition to reaction and fascism; for this position alone was proper to the fundamental humanitarian bent of his character. A further reason for the change in tone may have been the growing demands upon Thomas Mann's time made by his public activities. As one of the recognized leaders of the Germans in exile, and as editor of the magazine *Mass und Wert*, he found himself entering new circles and confronting new tasks. Moreover, at this very time he was beginning to prepare for his removal to America by making extensive lecture tours in the United States.

Political factors come to the fore in the letters of the thirties. Thomas Mann writes, often with passionate engagement, of the struggle against National Socialism and of his ties with Germans in exile. A striking difference between these and the earlier letters is the abandonment of literary discussion — the field in which Amann was at his best. Thus, in sending the third volume of the Joseph novel to Amann, Thomas Mann casually dismisses the matter with a reference to his "extended jests," and he thanks Amann for the latter's evidently lengthy and detailed commentary on the work with a few words deploring the trouble he has caused his correspondent.[25] Thomas Mann also takes a far more gingerly attitude toward Amann's manuscripts, a good many of which reached him at this time. His attitude is, in fact, distinctly negative, since it is now a question of publication in his own magazine—whereas during the World War years he exerted himself considerably to bring about publication of the essays Amann submitted to him. On the other hand he sincerely regretted the banning of Amann's *Tradition und Weltkrise,* in the first place because he obviously respected it as a literary achievement, and in the second place because this fresh example of the highhandedness and ruthlessness of the Nazi authorities concerned him closely as a writer.

We are specially favored in regard to the letters of the third, the American period, because, as has been mentioned, we possess a considerable number of copies of Amann's letters. As against eleven letters and postcards from Thomas Mann during the years 1948–1952, there are copies of thirteen of Amann's letters, and one, dated May 29, 1955, written under the impact of Thomas Mann's Schiller Memorial Address. These letters have not been included in the present edition; they have, however, been drawn upon frequently in the notes to explain passages in the corresponding Mann letters.

The themes of these later letters of Amann's are largely literary. Amann discusses in detail, and with great force, the works of Thomas Mann. In addition, however, he touches upon a large number of extremely diverse topics—his experiences in teaching in American colleges, for example; the virtues and defects of the American character, illustrated by numerous examples; the cultural situation of France, Germany, and Italy; the nature of the countryside around Plattsburgh and Lake Champlain and the military history of that vicinity. All these matters and many more are touched upon in a sprightly hodge-podge; Amann displays in these letters a certain tendency to ramble from one association to the other, but his wealth of knowledge and ideas renders his digressions always interesting, and the cheerful serenity of his point of view makes them appealing. The nature of many of these letters seems well characterized by Thomas Mann's reference—with a hint of good-natured irony—to Amann's "flow of lively talk." [26]

To judge by the letters, Thomas Mann's attitude toward Amann at this time remained one of sincere and equable sympathy. No doubt Amann's loyal enthusiasm for the other man's writing, and probably also the shared experience of exile, contributed to this friendliness. Thomas Mann's affability is most marked in his manner of responding to numerous details in Amann's letters, although he also frequently apologizes for the brevity of his own replies. Of particular value to us is Thomas

Mann's response to Amann's literary commentary. Thus Mann discusses Amann's comparison between *Doctor Faustus* and *Jean-Christophe;* his doubts as to whether composers and musicians can by their very nature be as cold and withdrawn from life as they are represented in *Doctor Faustus;* and especially Amann's reports on his extensive research into the personality of Friedrich Wilhelm Riemer, who plays so important a part in *The Beloved Returns.* Mann also occasionally confides something of the progress of his literary work—as, for example, when he speaks of the bouts of despair he underwent during the writing of *Doctor Faustus,* and of the difficulty he had in beginning anything new after the completion of that novel.

In these later letters political subjects are conspicuous by their absence. One letter of 1945, dealing with the chaotic state of Europe under the immediate impact of those restive days, is not printed here. Apart from this, Mann's only political commentary is the mention (in response to a remark of Amann's) of the result of the 1948 Presidential election in the United States, and a casual allusion to the crossing of the thirty-eighth parallel in Korea.[27]

So much for the history of the correspondence and the specific character of its various phases. In summary it may be said that the link between the two correspondents was based upon an exchange of ideas; and that it remained essentially an epistolary relationship. A proposed personal meeting in 1917 failed to come about—the fault being on both sides, as is evident from Letter 23. The first meeting between the two men did not take place until twenty years later, as Frau Dora Amann has kindly informed us. This was in 1937, in the course of a visit Thomas Mann paid to Vienna. There was only one more meeting, in 1941 or 1942, at the Quaker center in Haverford, Pennsylvania. However, there did exist on both sides a genuine epistolary friendship—at times, at any rate. Numerous details in the style and content of the letters testify to this.

At the request of Frau Katja Mann one entire letter has been omitted from this collection—the above-mentioned letter of 1945—and a total of eight passages from other letters. The length of these passages varies from two pages to mere clauses amounting to less than a line. We indicate such omissions in the text by a larger number of dots than the three occasionally used by Thomas Mann as marks of punctuation, and by footnote references. The numbered notes, explaining passages in the letters or citing parallels in the works of Thomas Mann, are printed in a special section after the letters.

IN CONCLUSION, the staff of the Municipal Library of Lübeck wishes to express its gratitude to all those who have contributed to the making of this edition. Our thanks are due first of all to Frau Katja Mann for graciously permitting the publication of her husband's letters. We wish to thank also Frau Dr. Luise Klinsmann of Lübeck, a personal friend of Frau Mann, for her kind intermediary offices in the negotiations. We are indebted to Frau Dora Amann for consent to print the draft of Paul Amann's letter of 1915, and for her patience and helpfulness in replying to a number of questions which her husband unhappily was no longer able to answer. We must again record our thanks to Paul Amann who, as we have mentioned, supplied us with a wealth of valuable data in the course of two full years of correspondence with him. In addition we wish to thank Dr. Robert Diehl, Professor Hermann Glockner, Dr. Arthur Hübscher, Professor Wolfgang F. Michael of the University of Texas; also the Frier Deutscher Hofstift [Frankfurt Goethe Museum], the Romanisches Seminar of the University of Kiel, the Deutsche Bücherei in Leipzig, the Westdeutsche Bibliothek in Marburg, the Bayerische Stattsbibliothek in Munich, the Accademia Nazionale dei Lincei in Rome, the Universitätsbibliothek in Tübingen, the Thüringische Landesbibliothek in Weimar, and the Osterreichische Nationalbibliothek in Vienna. Finally we are indebted to Hedwig Wegener for her careful assistance in the preparation of the text and notes.

HERBERT WEGENER

[*Lübeck,* 1959.]

The Letters

◄[1]►

Poschinger Strasse 1 [1]
Munich
February 2, 1915

My dear sir:

I have received your thought-provoking letter [2] and have read it through carefully several times. My sincere thanks.

It is not easy for me to say what I think of my *Rundschau* article.[3] It seems to me the classic remark that only the onlooker has scruples, while the man of action is always unscrupulous,[4] applies to the artist in a special and inverse fashion. We are scrupulous as actors (shapers, creators) because our mode of action is so high and serene that it possesses the dignity and coolness of contemplation. But since we know that the truth can only be given embodiment, never be spoken ("whenever he *speaks,* man must for the moment become one-sided" [5]), observation easily turns to action in us, and as spectators we are therefore unscrupulous. Without doubt some measure of this unscrupulousness is contained in my essay. It was an action sprung from rage, sprung from the simplistic, if you will, but urgent need to come to the intellectual rescue of my reviled nation—and, moreover, using dialectical methods borrowed from the others, from "civilization." [6] For my heart is German; but a rather

33

strong admixture of Latin American blood [7] gives me the power also to do what the Parisian rhetoricians and lawyers can do. I have never been a chauvinist, never a flatterer. I am aware of how much there is to criticize in the nature of the German. I love German self-criticism,[8] which is more serious and more unsparing, far more a necessity and passion and far less a luxury, than that of any other people. But think what this nation—let us speak softly, but incisively and distinctly: a nation such as this—has had to put up with, in word and deed, since the beginning of the war! Such things, I should think, were bound to rouse the most aloof individualist to a sense of national solidarity, national partisanship.[9] At least that is what happened to me. As for justice, if you will forgive the parliamentary expression, it was farcimentum [10] to me.

For really, what is justice! You write to me in the interests of being just—and are just only toward the enemy. The fact is that we are in opposition to one point of view or another.[11] The proper name for the golden mean is apathy. The fact that an Austrian today is in a better position than a German [12] to be just toward the enemy has its underlying reasons in history. Still and all, whatever need be said, over and above my poor article, in behalf of the German cause, need not be said to Germans, need not be said to Austrians. Hence a paragraph-by-paragraph reply to your letter, such as I at first felt tempted to write, is altogether superfluous.

In place of the much, the so much that might be said, permit me to make one comment. It concerns Romain Rolland.[13] "The soaring genius of his people," you say, "carries him into the thin atmosphere of heights in which we cannot yet breathe, and where he is preparing a home for our great-grandchildren." That would be greatly to "our" discredit—if it were so. "In this fateful moment he liberates himself forever from State and patriots," you say. Far from it—he has never been more, never so wholly a Frenchman. It is the gesture of Victor Hugo that he is making.[14] *"Montons dans le soleil et embrassons nous y!"*—an extremely Gallic gesture which, however, can all too easily be reconciled with other highly contradictory gestures. For example, with that of the old gentleman Anatole France, that blandly nihilistic graybeard who has just congratulated a Lisbon "Academy" for a statement composed of idiotic defamations of Germany.[15] What then? Then is Anatole France also, the pride of France, a discredit to Rolland, since he too obviously cannot yet breathe in that thin atmosphere? And does Rolland's love of mankind come to a halt before the people of Gogol—since he salutes the German troops who are fighting against the Cossacks? [16] I for my part confess that I bear far less of a grudge against Russia (necessary as it is to defeat her) than against our dear neighbors in the West. The Russian expansionist urge has something elemental and irresponsible about it, like the stretching motions and fearsome appetite of an awakening giant. The Western powers, on the other hand, must be measured by civilized standards; they are humanly responsible, humanly guilty. They have betrayed Europe by refusing to recognize Germany, refusing to grant her a little space on earth, and scheming against her [17] until she had to strike. I too had thought that a Franco-German agreement, a Franco-German *alliance,* must be the salvation of Europe, the goal of all policy, and even the goal of this war, when it had come. But, good God, how has France conducted herself! *"Raison"* has not prevented her from behaving like a naughty child who cries out for a whipping. Things will have to be made worse for her, much worse than they are today, for her to come to her senses.

Enough and too much—since I cannot say everything! I owe you thanks for the intellectual stimulus and, I may say, enrichment which your letter gave me. I dare not hope to perform a similar service for you with an essay on Frederick II and the coalition of 1756 [18] which I wrote recently. Nevertheless, accept it in a friendly spirit. Perhaps it will surprise you—at least to a certain extent.

I should be very happy if you would keep me informed on what fate holds in store for you. I send you my sincere good wishes and regards.

THOMAS MANN.

◄[2]►

Poschinger Strasse 1
Munich
March 25, 1915

My dear sir:

I have not yet thanked you for your second letter,[1] which was as rich as the first, let alone for your friendly comments on my Frederick essay.[2] That is very wrong of me. But I beg you to be forbearing, and not to misinterpret the scantiness of my replies. My health has always been rather unstable, and this conditions and constrains the realization of my wishes and thoughts more than ever these days; it is not boasting when I say that I am spiritually overburdened by events. On the contrary, that means simply that my capacity for work is poorly adapted to the tasks that the times impose upon heart and brain. The *Merkur* article [3] has little to do with the matters that worry me; it is not fundamental, was merely a way of keeping busy. But it has met with an uncommonly good reception, and since the *Merkur* does not reach a large audience, I have wanted to publish it again as a pamphlet. However, my Berlin publisher [4] is reluctant, since he fears giving offense and a misuse of the article abroad. Is he right? I do not think so. The people who might take offense would be people who do not matter, and the political damage would be superficial and insignificant compared to the intellectual respect which should be felt abroad for German desire for self-knowledge. My own scruples against any wider distribution of the article turn rather in precisely the opposite direction. When all is said and done, what is glorified in the article, though glorified in a sly and skeptical fashion, is Prussianism. And I see very well that after this war Prussianism, politically speaking, will belong to the past. It will no longer play any essential part in Germany's *future,* whose greatness remains a certainty to me.[5] There can no longer be any doubt that the spirit of Prussianism has fulfilled its task for Germany; it is destined to be supplanted. What I sincerely wish is that this supplanting may not take place in a catastrophic manner, with accompanying abuse and abasement. It horrifies me that revolutionary sloganizing on the one hand and the commercial spirit on the other might conquer the Prussian spirit and shatter Germany inwardly. Were that to happen, the nation could be severely shaken and thrown off course in its faith in itself. And that must not be—for the sake of Germany's and Europe's future.[6]

You have no doubt read attentively, as I have, Sir Edward Grey's [7] last speech in the House of Commons. I do not think it had any special political intent; it came from the heart, although from a heart filled with *cant*.* No,[8] Prussia-Germany has never taught that Might is Right. She has at most and at worst taught, and acted accordingly, that necessity knows no law, and that Right —is Might. This pessimistic philosophy of Right has been imposed upon her by the world over centuries of political humiliation and impotence. For a long time Germany was wholly devoted to thought. She awoke late to reality, and when she began to look around on earth she found that Right was in fact Might.[9] She brutalized herself—out of intellectuality.[10] She had been quick to perceive that only in the materials of the mind, in art, in philosophy, thought is capable of achieving radical concretization.[11] (What came of the revolution? The capitalistic bourgeois republic. A pretty mess!) Germany was radical in the mind, but never cared to be so in reality. (In this lies her lack of open-spiritedness, of childlike trust!) Bismarck's *Realpolitik* and imperial structure correspond to Luther's concessions, to Kant's "practical

* The word *cant* in English in the original.

38

reason." [12] The German love of reality is ironically melancholic, rather gloomy and rather brutal.[13] It does not have radicalism's gallantry of gesture. In the final analysis it is not without contempt. For that reason the world refuses to grant it free play—the world which is filled with *cant* and defends the empty gestures and empty phrases of humanitarian optimism against this German realism. What I would like to see is this: that with the discarding of political Prussianism, with the democratization of Germany [14] which obviously will be the consequence of this war, Germany may be stripped of her gloom without becoming shallow; that her relationship to reality may take a more intimate and happy form, so that she can lead the way to a democratic world culture —for the leadership must not fall to America.

> With all best regards,
> Sincerely yours,
> THOMAS MANN.

⋆[3]⋆

> Poschinger Strasse 1
> Munich
> June 13, 1915

My dear Herr Doktor:

Many thanks for your letter from Budapest (where last year I spent several most enjoyable, stimulating days). You put me to shame with what you say about our correspondence. I am only too well aware that you

39

are the giver, and in the final analysis perhaps that is quite in order. Is the artist an intellectual being at all? Perhaps he cannot be, because he is to so high a degree a person who simultaneously shapes and wills. I doubt that the stock of human thought has ever been enriched by artists. In fact Nietzsche contends that artists have always been merely the lackeys of some morality or other [1] and firmly refuses to take them seriously as intellectuals. A great many things might be said concerning the relationship of intellect to art. At best the two will supplement one another in an exchange, but even so, intellect will owe no debt of gratitude to art.

I sincerely hope that our contact will never again completely be broken off, and would like to ask you (as I think I have already done) to keep me up to date, when you are in the field too, by dropping me a few lines from time to time.

My best wishes go with you. That you are confident of a happy return is to me an excellent augury. With faith in this, I gladly pledge myself to do my utmost to further the publication of your writings. If however fate should hold something else in store for you, I shall consider myself honor bound to be the guardian of your work.

Once more, all good wishes!
Yours sincerely,
THOMAS MANN.

◄ 4 ►

Poschinger Strasse 1
Munich
August 3, 1915

Dear sir:

Your last letter—dated June 20!—is still lying un-
answered on my desk—things at home during the past
weeks have been as unfavorable as possible to any serious
correspondence. Have I already told you of the illness
that descended upon my family? Three children and
finally my wife herself were stricken with appendicitis
—now is that contagion or not? The doctors admit the
infectious character of the disease, but say that it cannot
be contagious, which in the light of our case strikes me
as pigheaded. With the eldest boy,[1] the thing had all
possible complications: peritonitis, repeated abscesses,
intestinal stoppage, intestinal paralysis. Some terrible
operations had to be performed; we had all but given up
hope. But the little heart, strong in its youthfulness, held
out, and today the boy can stand unsupported on his legs,
though the poor little legs are as thin as sticks. Day after
tomorrow we shall be able to take him to Tölz (Bad Tölz
in the Isar Valley) where we have a cottage . . .[2]

August 7. I was interrupted and now *am* already
in Tölz, in my tiny study with its ingenuous view out on
meadow, valleys, and spruce woods. One of these interminable Bavarian rains is falling.

How are things with you, what is your life like? As
contemplative as it was in June, when you told me about

Condorcet? [3] Ah yes, how many things there are on both sides of the way that tempt us and cry out to be given form. But one has to go straight ahead; one has no choice. I never had, and in the three youthful years during which I heaped up [4] *Buddenbrooks* I once and for all learned renunciation and steadiness of the eye. More than any other human being, the artist learns that life is renunciation and limitation; nowhere is his humanness more marked than in this . . . Before the war [5] I had begun a longish story [6] whose scene was a sanatorium for tuberculosis in the high mountains—a story with pedagogic and political overtones, in which a young man comes up against the most seductive of powers, death, and runs the gauntlet, in a comic-gruesome manner, of the intellectual polarities of Humanism and Romanticism, progress and reaction, health and disease; but not so much that he may be forced to decide, as for the sake of orientation and general enlightenment. The spirit of the whole is humoristically nihilistic, and the bias leans rather toward the side of sympathy with death. [7] *The Magic Mountain* [8] is its name, and there is something in it of the dwarf for whom seven years pass like so many days. For conclusion, for resolution—I see no other possibility but the outbreak of the war. As a storyteller one cannot ignore this reality, and I believe I have some right to it, since the premonition of it has been in all my conceptions. [9] Look at *Death in Venice!* Good or bad—but is there a book that could stand in its place as more pertinent to the times? [10] Incidentally the same may be said of a good many writings of the past few years. I am, of course, greatly hindered by the events of the day and my improvisations on historical and political themes, and am lagging far behind schedule. At the same time, moreover, *The Magic Mountain* is in itself only an interpolation [11]—for its sake I interrupted a novel of which only a third is finished: *Confessions of Felix Krull* [12]— a horribly strange undertaking, the caricature of great autobiography and in the style itself a parody of [Goethe's] *Poetry and Truth*,[13] but in the end arriving at something new in its distorted lyricism. As soon as I have knocked off *The Magic Mountain*—and that will be a long while yet—I must once again bow under that foolish yoke. And all the while current developments give head and heart so infinitely much to do, so much to cope with, that at this moment I do not know whether I can and should go on telling tales, or whether I must pull myself together for a thoroughgoing, sober discussion, a coming to terms on a personal and self-analytic basis with the burning problems of the day. For what I have hitherto attempted along these lines is in my eyes also, and for my needs, extremely inadequate. The *Rundschau* essay of which you heard was a letter to the *Svenska Dagbladet;* it appeared there in Swedish, in answer to a questionnaire that they were sending around.[14] Thus it was the fulfillment of a journalistic obligation, nothing more. Since then I have written a few lines for the August 1 issue of the *Frankfurter Zeitung* [15] which likewise would not be worthwhile sending to you, quite aside from the question of whether you would like it, whether its bias would appeal to you.

Forgive me! But I ask myself how you can reconcile the final phrases of your letter, the confident expectation that everything must ultimately turn out well—well for Germany—with the conviction that Germany represents romanticism and reaction and that the French principle of revolution will dominate the *future* (the entire, the whole future?!). For the curious aspect of the matter is that we all at bottom believe in the war, regard it as a judgment of God, and are prepared to accept its verdict as beyond appeal. And since according to your conviction the future belongs to the ideas of the Entente—I mean the Western ideas, which are also those of liberal Russia—you ought therefore to count on Germany's defeat as a certainty. Or does an erroneous, contrary to sense, anti-ideal outcome of the war seem conceivable to you? Not to me, not for a moment. Rather I am profoundly convinced that France—France seen in the large, historically—is today without any mission, any task, is blind to the times, condemned, disoriented, hopeless; that it is fighting a dead and from any but the heroic point of view superfluous battle, and that all historic justice, all real modernity, future, certainty of victory, lie with Germany. Otherwise would it not be the first time in all history that ideas which a hundred years ago stood for victory, youth, the future, would always stand for these, time and again, even after they had had their triumph? Do not the Western powers strike us today as predominantly *old,* in fact old-fashioned? Insofar as they represent achieved imperialistic and cultural goals, they seem aristocratic, and I believe that a good deal of the sympathy for the West which flourishes among us, allegedly for democratic elements, is in truth sympathy for the aristocratic, sympathy with old, noble, vanishing worlds:

is romanticism, "sympathy with death." The West is old, naïve, and refined; it is eighteenth-century in its humanism, ideology, and phraseology; its ideas are those of the bourgeois revolution, of the literary spirit, of the emancipation of the Third Estate—and nothing more. All old hat nowadays.[16] To be sure, the new element which Germany hopes to put to use in shaping the future is difficult to define at present, since it is not a thing to be put into words but is inherent in deeds. The slogan the old fogies have picked up is "organization," [17] and this does in fact say what really counts today and in the next century. For, don't you agree, in the last analysis it is nothing less than the *social reorganization of Europe* that counts—a task which is obviously beyond the aptitude of the West and which, equally obviously, constitutes the mission of Germany . . . But I see very well that I am speaking boldly of things somewhat beyond my scope. The pretty part of it is that Germany represents Western refinement, too, in part, that is vis à vis the East, in the area where you are fighting. Let me hear from you again if you are not annoyed by my loquacity, which may be only oxygen intoxication, and please accept my best wishes and regards.

Sincerely yours,

THOMAS MANN.

◄[5]►

Tölz
September 10, 1915

Dear Herr Doktor:

First and foremost my heartiest wishes for your recovery.[1] Intestinal illness and lung catarrh! Really, don't you think you have had enough of the cruel game? Or are you thinking of going out again? In asking I assume that you have some degree of choice whether or not you go out. You have really done your share fully by now. And you do not seem especially prey to the fascination of war, as many are. But in the end you may well be back in the field again by the time you receive this note, which has been delayed by house guests and my being out of sorts from the continual bad weather—a note which even today, I fear, will be somewhat inadequate . . .

It is amazing how well you characterize the main intention of my last story.[2] I am all the more grateful to you for the formulation since it also covers fairly well the concluding idea of the new work [3] which is at present occupying me. It is too bad that the best critics do not engage in criticism; those who write our reviews and hand down their verdicts are chiefly rabble. As far as *Death in Venice* is concerned, I am scarcely a competent interpreter by now; I have almost forgotten the work. But I know this much, that I have almost universally been misunderstood in the crudest fashion. What was most painful to me was that the "hieratic atmosphere" was taken as a personal claim on my part [4]—whereas it was nothing but caricature.[5] The cultural Hellenism, too, was taken literally, whereas it was only an expedient and an intellectual refuge for the character. The nature of the whole is rather Protestant than classical. What I had dimly in mind was the problem of the artist's dignity, something like the tragedy of mastership; and the novella in fact grew out of an initial plan to tell the story of Goethe's last love: the seventy-year-old's passion for that little girl in Marienbad [6] (wasn't it?), whom he was determined to marry, which she and his family would not hear of—a shocking, grotesque, terrible story which, perhaps, in spite of "D.i.V." I am going to retell some day . . . But what a simple-minded idea most people have about "confessions"! When I deal with an artist, or even a master, I do not mean "me," I am not asserting that I am a master or even only an artist. I am merely saying that I *know* something about the nature of the artist and master. Nietzsche says somewhere: "To understand something about art, make a few works of art." And he considers the artists of the day as intermediaries between us and the great masters; they somehow catch and conduct the heat rays of the great masters of the past. When I examine myself closely I realize that this and this only has been the purpose of my "creativity": to acquire the sensibility of the masters.[7] It has been a game, just as I played "prince" [8] as a boy in order to acquire the princely sensibility. In the course of my literary labors I acquired access to knowledge about the existence of the artist, in fact of the great artist, and can therefore say something about it. I came by my insight into the existence of a reigning sovereign in the same way. In general: I speak far less of myself than of those things which my own existence permits me to *guess* at . . .

As I reread for the second and third time your intelligent, at once witty and completely considered remarks on revolution, on Germany, on Germany's incapacity to produce anything ideally new out of herself, I have to smile at the way I am compelled to disagree. Really, what in the world *am* I doing in this camp? [9] What am I, thoroughly antisocial, nihilistically unpolitical artist that I am, doing so warmly defending Germanism even on dubious points? War fever? No, it cannot be that. In the first place so easily enervated a person as myself could not sustain a state of intoxication for a whole year, and in the second place I am not one of those who had to be "given a good shaking up" by the outbreak of the war. On the contrary, I was well prepared, knew at once what was going on; all that had happened was that the things I had long ago felt, thought, and spoken of, socially at least, if not in writing, suddenly became urgent, burning issues, the call of the hour. Truly, I think that I am being objective, under no outside pressure and not merely patriotic when I disagree with you. I do not deceive myself about the fact that Germany has all of world liberalism against her—the liberal movement which is so dead certain that it means progress. The whole political Left is against Germany: in Bucharest, in Athens as in Rome; whereas all the conservative and retrograde powers sympathize with her, for example the papacy.[10] But this, I think, is misleading, and arises from a misunderstanding. If world liberalism [11] still represented progress, still had the future for itself, then it would scarcely have the whole world on its side and would not have penetrated even to the savages, who are already raving about "freedom." That "Western ideas" are still the leading, victorious, truly revolutionary ideas, is to my mind a superstition. I feel sure that progress, revolution, modernity, youth, newness, are with Germany to-day—in spite of all sorts of circumstances which complicate and obscure the actual situation—and feel sure that world liberalism will be defeated—no, is already defeated.

At times the justification for this belief seems obvious to me, and then again I see at other times that it is very difficult to prove. The best that I can say about it is that no kind of crude personal interest is influencing my views. Quite the contrary. The cause of the West is so thoroughly intertwined with literature, with the "literary spirit," that I really ought more or less to feel it as my own cause, or at least as the cause of the Latin literary man within myself . . . for such there is.[12] To put it crudely: an *amusing* [13] Europe, a "civilized" Europe in which the writer has some say, ought to be up my alley. If that is not the case, at least I cannot be blamed for egoism. I side with Bismarck in a distaste for literary politics, and in that I am anti-revolutionary.

Far be it from me to deprecate the French Revolution as a historical event. But little as I wish to make myself ridiculous, I cannot hide my true feelings about it. I do not share your love for revolution. I see in it so much of operatic gesture, inhuman sentimentality, lack of honest reservations, lack of love for truth and therefore lack of *freedom*, that my innermost soul is outraged. I am partly of Latin American blood [14] ; in intellectual matters I tend sometimes in the Romance direction; and in my creative work I have occasionally paid tribute to Latin aesthetistic rhetoric. But the political legalism, the Jacobinism and Freemasonry of the Latins, the spirit of the democratic doctrinaire and the tyrannical school-master of revolution,[15] is a horror to me. And in this war, which in any case separates the sheep from the goats, I have separated myself, probably forever, from the friends of the Allies within Germany: our radical literati, the "intellectuals" par excellence, who think they have a lease on "intellectuality" in general, whereas it is only the literary intellectuality of the bourgeois revolution that they know and mean [16]—all those belles-lettres politicians who today, believe me! are bitterly disappointed because the Anglo-French invasion, the physical and moral crushing of Germany by the West, will not come off . . . "Solidarity of all intellectuals" . . . I have never been surer that such a thing *does not exist*. Not that human tolerance in all matters of the human spirit is not possible and desirable. But it is radicalism that does not observe such tolerance . . .

This letter is swelling and yet as a treatise remains unbearably inadequate. Enough.

You are certainly right in saying that whatever of critical spirit has been present in Germany must not, after the war, perish in self-admiration. Only it would be desirable if the critical spirit, insofar as it is embodied in art, were able to push on beyond politics to the realm of ethical humanism; for in the first place the political alone can scarcely act as a liberating force in creative art, and in the second place "the others" have behaved in such a manner that we at least know this: They are no better than we.

With a plea for forbearance and with best wishes and regards,

Yours,

THOMAS MANN.

◦[6]◦

Tölz
October 1, 1915

Dear Professor Amann:

That was certainly a delightful packet! I can only poorly reciprocate by sending a photo of myself [1] which I received a few days ago. It is, it seems to me, a very successful portrait. The person who took it is a passionate camera fan, a Viennese incidentally. Kindly accept this print as a token of my fellow-feeling, respect, and gratitude.

As for your manuscript,[2] I have read it with deep emotion. I understand fully why you were impelled to set down so lovingly that painfully vital incident, so timely now in all its everyday intimacy and everyday tragedy. Every reader will understand and feel it as I did—most forcibly, I should think, the scholarly reader. I thought of the scholarly public of the *Frankfurter Zeitung* when I offered the manuscript to this newspaper

51

first of all. I should think it will be welcome there as a Sunday feature. The length may present an obstacle. In that case we shall look further.

May I keep the issue of *Effort*? [3] Your essay in it has given me great pleasure. You call your French "dubious," but it strikes me as completely convincing. Without having a perfect command of the language, I have an understanding of it, have something of its spirit in me (something like an uncultivated but gifted actor who, if you don't listen too closely, gives an astonishing performance of Riccaut), and the rhythm of your sentences seems to me absolutely genuine. Genuine above all are the delicacy, tenderness, sprightly sympathy with which your French treats—not to say caresses—literary matters. It often seems to me that French is the only language in which to talk about literature, and in reading your article this feeling of mine was confirmed anew. This language alone creates around literary art that atmosphere of knowledgeable respect and well-wishing which an art needs in order to thrive in self-confidence. For them, literature is the national art, as music is for us. For us, literature is something basically alien. A musician ought to be a German, and a writer a Frenchman, or they are only half-baked specimens. What power there is in language! If you had written your essay in German, you would scarcely have allotted the most space to *Royal Highness* among my works. This book can best be discussed in French, and perhaps only in French. I realized that at once when it was published—French reviewers found the story *charmant,* whereas German reviewers received it with deep disapproval.[4] A lady of superior attainments wished to know whether I was not ashamed to offer such a thing after *Buddenbrooks.* Critic after critic eschewed the task of reckoning how much art I had expended on this nonsense. The only one who *noticed* any higher aims was logically enough a Viennese, Hermann Bahr [5]—as indeed one senses at once the milder atmosphere, the mellower culture, as soon as one crosses the Austrian border.[6] At bottom the "Reich" is inhospitable to writers, most inhospitable. Have I not said that an "amusing" Europe, a Westernized literary Europe, would be up my alley? [7] If I were conceited, I would perhaps wish for an Allied victory. But there has always been too much irony in my temperament for me to be properly conceited . . .

A few days ago the original of Perceval,[8] our collie, whom we called "Motz" in moments of deep affection, passed away. That is to say, he was passed away. Since [9] the good and once so beautiful boy was suffering from an ugly skin disease for which the veterinary said there was no cure, and since he was also failing generally, we thought that his existence was no longer worthy of him, and had the local gunsmith dispatch him with two good bullets, one in the spine and one in the head to make doubly sure. He died instantly. We are glad that we did not entrust the comrade of a decade to the "knacker" [10] —a creature whom we endow in our imaginations with the most repulsive traits. For now Motz rests from all his noble-spirited madnesses in a respectable grave on the edge of the woods, behind our garden. The children, with whom he was close friends, have placed flowers on the grave, nor have we omitted to give him a stone, a field boundary stone that has served its day and now bears the simple inscription of his name.[11] The portrait I drew of him [12] was quite accurate and realistic, and it fitted easily and happily into the story, as I well recall. I thought it appropriate to inform you of his decease.

Your letter has once more been a source of stimulus and instruction to me—and of embarrassment as well. For I cannot read without feeling embarrassed that you wish to throw yourself into the front a third time—you who obviously take far less an affirmative view of this war than do I, who am still at home and presumably will remain at home. Fortunately I can say that I have only approved the war since it has come. I am no Gabriele,[13] no blood-and-thunder aesthete,[14] have not had the shamelessness to advocate the war; rather I honestly thought it could not be for ethical reasons. (Curious, is it not, that "intellect" is not necessarily pacifistic; in Italy it made the war.) [15] A non-serving militiaman par excellence, I have always had only symbolic relations to soldiering. My call-up at the beginning of the war was marked by utmost corruption.[16] The army doctor, a man who plain to see was an utter civilian and blindly devoted to the fine arts, fell into a delighted flutter of respect as soon as he heard my name, and promptly exempted me on physical grounds "so that I would be let alone." [17] (Literally.) A thoroughly un-German case of bribery by literature. But after all the man was right. There would not be much sense for me to participate physically. My nerves are poor, I really just barely manage to "hold" myself in line, my digestive apparatus, my head, my heart, would rapidly fail me, and for psychological reasons I should prefer to be spared making a fool of myself in the face of reality. Incidentally, a new call-up of those who had been mustered out has been initiated. Men over forty are temporarily excepted, but if the war should go on I may still expect to be plunged into some sort of adventure.

What do you think about the situation? It is grave, it seems to me. Mackensen [18] is not breaking through, the encirclement has probably failed, and the tempest in the East may be more dangerous than our press admits. At any rate it is a hard, hard struggle—and that is good for Germany, much better than a swift, triumphal victory would have been [19]—though that, incidentally, lay beyond the realm of possibility from the first, in the face of this coalition. Although the certainty of Germany's victory has always been firmly with me—I have moments when I am horrified, when I doubt. Here in Germany we underestimate the inner conviction of our foes, their belief in their right, their cause, their mission, their duty to protect Europe from Germany. If it is their earnest will, resolved to the utmost, not to let Germany win—is winning then humanly possible? And is a German victory that costs such a price even desirable? For my part I should take little pleasure in belonging to a nation that has its foot upon the neck of Europe. That would not be very nice, and I believe that on the whole the German soul would find it unbearable. Imagine the situation after the peace if we keep northern France under occupation for decades in order to exploit it and so recover our financial losses, which could not be done otherwise. I am not concerned about France. France could have remained neutral. And yet such a state of affairs would be uncomfortable to the point of being unbearable for every sensitive person among us, and I cannot help thinking that the very knowledge of such a thing would necessarily have a demoralizing, brutalizing effect upon our people, more brutalizing than the war. Nevertheless we *must* regain what we have spent if we aren't to starve. The solution of this problem is more difficult than victory itself.

I would be glad to hear your opinion on a thought that occurred to me again while reading your *Effort* article. When I suggest this matter to Austrians, they tend to be delighted. But Austrians are too easily delighted. A great deal has been said about a German-Austrian economic *rapprochement* after the war, a closer bond between the two states. How would it be if we had a cultural symbol that would demonstrate plainly to the world the closeness of this bond, in which the linguistic element plays a considerable part—I mean, how would it be to have a *German Academy in Vienna?* I have often toyed with [20] the thought of an official German academy for the honor and advancement of literature; the war has given me the idea that the seat of this institution must necessarily be Vienna. One part of me acclaims the idea; another protests against it. The former is no doubt the man of letters in me, the latter—the creative writer. But where such a dualism is possible, is an academy possible? Let me hear your opinion!

All the best wishes for your recovery.

Sincerely yours,
THOMAS MANN.

⚜ 7 ⚜

Poschinger Strasse 1
Munich
October 21, 1915

Dear Professor Amann:

I have just received your friendly note with your new address, and am at once sending the proofs [1] which have been here with me for some days. Please look to them right away and send them to the *Frankfurter Zeitung,* which is waiting for them!

The photo was accompanied by a lengthy letter.[2] Have you not received it? I also sent a card after it, concerning your essay. Mail service is frightfully slow— your letter is dated the 14th! Please drop me a line at once to inform me of the arrival of these things. I am somewhat concerned.

With cordial greetings,
Sincerely yours,
THOMAS MANN.

⚜ 8 ⚜

Poschinger Strasse 1
Munich
November 7, 1915

Dear Professor:

For the present I can only thank you in the briefest fashion for your fine, stimulating letter of October 17.

I have plunged into a critical—essayistic—work, a kind of essay, or no, they are almost private scribblings, which attempt to create a fusion—a strange and rash experiment—between contemporary events and a revision of my personal point of view. The effort is a considerable psychological strain upon me. At the moment I am absolutely unfit for writing letters. Make allowances! and in any case keep me informed about your welfare and your address.

Most cordial regards,
Yours,
THOMAS MANN.

⟨ 9 ⟩

Munich
February 25, 1916

Dear Doctor:

I read your essay,[1] including the preface, at once, have reread several parts, and hasten to tell you that I love and admire this work with all my heart. You know that I am not so attached to your subject as you are; before the war I had no distinct image of Rolland's personality; only during the war did I acquire some perspective on it, and then he seemed to me all too spiritual, all to officiously humanitarian, without a deeper feeling for the fatefulness and necessity of a scourge and an upheaval which in the final analysis must correspond to the common will of all Europe. To call it a "crime against humanity," as Mr. Sasonow [2] has just done again, is to treat it far too shallowly. Rolland's *Au-dessus de la mêlée* [3] contains much that is fine and lovable, but the title remains a self-deception, it seems to me, and I agree with St. George who, so I am told, has characterized the book as at bottom "foolishly French." Can you find any passage in it which is really just toward the German character? How significant that he translates the really passionately felt German watchword of the beginning of the war, *Not,* by *nécessité!* [4] Correctly enough, of course. But *nécessité,* my God, that is nothing at all. *Nécessité* is a rational recognition of a fact, but *Not* is supreme creative pathos. It was Richard Wagner's favorite word . . . Nevertheless, why has your study been such a benefaction to me? Why have I devoured it so eagerly? It is difficult to say. In some elusive manner it suits my mood, meets my needs, which are by no means the same as they were several months ago. I am exceedingly tired of the hatred, the accusations, the excited self-assertiveness, tired of the "war"; I am deeply inclined toward softness, peace, even toward penitence. Thought has soonest fought to exhaustion . . . [5] Perhaps I am a little anticipating Europe's state of mind *afterward.* Our error was to imagine that this was a "war," an incident after which everything would be approximately the same as before. But it is rather an upheaval of all inner and outer things, a total revolution which cannot be compared with the revolution of 1789 without overestimating the latter. At the end of this upheaval there will be no "victory," no decision for one of the two parties. It was an illusion that there are any parties, any "enemies" in this conflict. The truth is that all nations together, obeying a higher decree, are laboring for the renewal and rebirth of Europe, of the European soul. That will be recognized late, but ultimately, and only on the basis of this insight will reconciliation be possible—on a *religious* basis, then; odd though the word seems to me, I feel it. I believe that I can feel in my nerves and in my emotions something of the Europe that will be afterward: an exhausted Europe, but nevertheless one full of youthful hope, sensitive, purified and appeased by common suffering, reconciled, inclined toward a tender spirituality, undoctrinaire, unself-righteous, for all the older antitheses and slogans will have become outmoded. Poor, of course, poor and idealistic, poor and decent, utterly divorced from the primitive pleasure-seeking, the civilized crudity, of the past.[6]

I suppose I am being starry-eyed, for according to all we hear, no sooner will the war on the battlefield be over when it will be replaced at once by an even fiercer commercial war. But I only wanted to suggest to you the mood in which your splendid essay found me, and how closely it corresponded with this mood. Since I began this letter in the evening and continued it in the morning, another day has come, and I have meanwhile read the manuscript straight through a second time. (I am even afraid I have disfigured it with pencil marks [7]; if it is spoiled, I want to take care of the damage.) Yes, it should certainly be published now! How? Where? That, to be sure, is a delicate question. I am not certain that it would fit into the framework of a monthly. Is it not too long? Perhaps you could do without the longer quotations—though I suggest this reluctantly. But to what publication to submit it? The *Süddeutsche Monatshefte* are too aggressively German. The *Weisse Blätter* [8] would undoubtedly publish it with pleasure, if their space at all permitted. But the thing is that I would not want them to have it. There, where my brother Heinrich's famous Zola article has already appeared,[9] a tour de force of double meaning in which we are given to understand that this war is a kind of European Dreyfus trial, a struggle between the "saber" and "truth and justice" (Germany is the "saber," [10] of course)—there your essay would no longer have the proper effect or taste: they already have a burnt palate there.[11] What I would like is for it to be published in the *Neue Rundschau,* my favorite periodical [12] ; its appearance there would dispel any impression that may have arisen that the war has caused serious damage to the soul of the magazine.[13] Would you allow me some time? In March, probably during the first half of the month, I shall be going to Berlin for a few days. I should like to take the manuscript with me then and work for it on the spot to the best of my ability. Do you consent?

I am extremely grateful to you for everything that your essay has taught me about young France. Since my command of the language is deficient, my knowledge was not much more than a vague feeling. Now I see more clearly. My desire to appreciate and to admire is very strong; but the official France of this war has repelled and embittered me more than I can say—and then I have had to hear my own brother talking exactly like Monsieur Deschanel [14] or Monsieur Hanotaux! [15] What

I despise is the Jacobin, the doctrinaire of liberty, the bourgeois rhetorician, whether he wears the garb of French revolutionary or Italian Freemason. But I have always known that there was another France, and when I read Claudel's *L'annonce faite à Marie*,[16] first in German and then in the original, I was enchanted.

You ask about the treatise that I mentioned to you.[17] It goes badly. I have poured out everything, scribbled away some two hundred quarto pages—and do not know what I should do with them, for publicly none of it is possible—that is to say, objectively it is, but subjectively, for me, no longer possible. "Each of our thoughts is only a moment of our lives. Of what use would life be to us if not to correct our errors, to conquer our prejudices, and daily to make our heart and thoughts more expansive? . . . We use every day to acquire a little more of truth." [18] That is what I am in the habit of reminding the know-it-alls; whoever thinks he has hold of the truth cannot be a lover of truth. In his war book [19] Rolland says that the intellectuals in the present war have been more violently infected by the bellicose spirit than others. *"J'ajoute (c'est leur punition),"* he continues, *"qu'ils en restent plus longtemps victimes: car tandis que les simple gens, soumis à l'épreuve incessante de l'action journalière et de leurs expériences, se modifient avec elles et le font sans remords, les intellectuels se trouvent liés dans le filet de leur esprit, et chacun de leurs écrits leur est un lien de plus."* *

---

* I may add (and this is their punishment) that they remain longer in its bondage: for while ordinary people, constantly put to the test as they are by their experiences and by everyday life,

I may say that this does not apply to me in the least, for the reason that I am at bottom as little of an intellectual in Rolland's sense as Rolland himself. I shall never become the slave of my thoughts, for I know that nothing merely thought and said is true, and that only *form* is unassailable. When I indulge in writing, by first motto is: *"Ihr müsst mich nicht durch Widerspruch verwirren. Sobald man spricht, beginnt man schon zu irren."* [20] [You must not confound me with my inconsistencies. As soon as we speak, we begin to err.] And my second: "But as soon as our thought has found words, it is no longer sincere, *nor in the profoundest sense serious.*" (Schopenhauer.) I am so far from fettering myself intellectually with my *écrits* that the exposition of my ideas in writing is my only means of getting rid of them, passing beyond them to other, newer, better, and if possible altogether contrary ideas—*sans remords!* Thus the whole intellectual reckoning-up of which I wrote you (the labor of several months) now bores me frightfully, and only out of a sense of order and a bourgeois disinclination to "let anything go to waste" will I probably pull together what I have written and attempt to make something usable out of it. The core of the matter for me is the intellectualization, politicalization, democratization of Germany and of German literature, which is now being wildly advocated in certain quarters. Well, my nature has always been, if only by inheritance, more inclined toward intellectual Europeanism than poetic German-

---

change with these experiences, readily and without compunction, the intellectuals are chained by their minds, and each of their writings adds a link to their chains.

ism; but from the point of view of individualistic libertarianism I have one or two protests to make.

With cordial regards,
Yours,
THOMAS MANN.

❧[10]❧

Munich
March 17, 1916

Dear Professor:

I am just on my feet again after a bout of influenza that passed fairly quickly but was very violent while it lasted—never in my life have I had so high a fever—and I am still thoroughly shaken from it and fear that I will go on feeling the effects for weeks to come. Thus the Berlin lecture trip has become problematical—I have not yet canceled it, but shall probably do so, and must therefore renounce my intention of handing in your manuscript [1] personally. I have dispatched it by mail, along with a lengthy and, I hope, effective letter in which I have in your name given permission for condensations, omission of quotations, et al. I have also left it to the editors to use or omit the foreword—so that the piece will not be rejected because of its length. I am as eager to see the essay in the *Rundschau* as if it were an article of my own.

I have received your two letters of the first and the eleventh with the greatest pleasure—and am particularly grateful for the photo, which struck me as utterly right and inevitable, as though I had always seen you that way in my mind. The brow is clear and sensible; underneath, in spite of the semi-smile of exposure [2] many signs of strain and pain, indicating that you do not have too easy a life.

If only my strength will come back soon. My head is very bad and weak. Other people run temperatures of 102° every time they have a cold, but for me, who never have fever, it was something altogether extraordinary which has ridiculously sapped my strength. As yet I can scarcely think of working, for which reason I am enormously bored. The worst is that although my taste buds behave normally for eating and drinking, I cannot *smoke* because it "tastes" bad—which can only be due to some weakness of the nerves. Or what else? Do you know anything about the matter? I try again and again, because I *miss* the stimulus terribly, but it won't do. I observed the same phenomenon once before in the mountains, in Davos; there too, during the first week, with body temperature slightly above normal, my taste for smoking vanished.[3] Have you any explanation for that? It drives me to distraction. I smoke moderately, but passionately.

With all best wishes and regards,

Yours,

THOMAS MANN.

Good that nowadays we can open a letter to Austria again without ruining the stamp. I have not yet thanked you for your Fontane study,[4] although I have read it with the greatest pleasure and profit. The subject is dear and close to me.[5] I have scarcely ever found it so interestingly treated.

◦⟦ 11 ⟧◦

March 26, 1916

Congratulations on the fulfillment of your wish! The influenza was followed by erysipelas; I am up again today for the first time. The Rolland is being read in Berlin now.

Yours,

Thomas Mann.

◦⟦ 12 ⟧◦

Tölz

April 15, 1916

Dear Professor:

It is vexing; your manuscript has come back from Berlin, although with the most complimentary comments. They "find the qualities of the author outstanding." He "writes so well and finely" that they would like to ask him "to undertake something else for us." But such a large essay on Rolland cannot be given a place now; it bears too much the mark of having been written "before the war"; perhaps the author will be willing to wait until all of Jean-Christophe has appeared in German; then it might

66

be considered again, etc. I have now—in fact two weeks ago—handed the manuscript in to the *Neuer Merkur* in Munich, the periodical published by Müller, in which my essay on Frederick first appeared. However, the editor is off traveling at present, and so the decision will probably take a while. Nevertheless, I am glad that the editors of *Rundschau* have made your literary acquaintance. Their request for something else is undoubtedly intended seriously. You will find open doors there.

We have been here for a week. It was summer when we came, and now a sleety snow is falling outside my window. I am still somewhat shaky (did I write that after the influenza I had erysipelas?), but I can live and put in at least two hours work daily, which for me is very important. My treatise is in a sense a reply to a literary-political type whom I have called the "civilization literati," [1] and who are promulgating the literarization, radicalization, intellectualization, politicalization—in short, the democratization of Germany—a development that is perhaps inevitable, but toward which I find myself in a certain conservative opposition. There is much to be said —though one cannot possibly say everything anyhow, and precisely because direct speech is not really my business, I always want to say everything.

With best wishes and regards,
Yours,
THOMAS MANN.

⋅[13]⋅

Tölz
Easter Sunday, 1916 [1]

Dear Professor:

Your friendly letter of the 15th has reached me safely. Have you received mine, informing you of the temporary fate of your manuscript? [2] I am not certain whether I addressed it to Vienna or to Hungary—the former would no doubt have been better.

How vividly and temptingly you describe your new environment. I know nothing of the Near East, let alone the farther and far. Although I often feel a powerful hunger for the world, I am on the whole a mushroom that stays put, [3] to speak with Schopenhauer, and actually alternate only between Munich and Tölz—we call our little city house the Winter Palace, and Tölz bears the name Tsarskoye-Selo. [4] Venice remains the most unusual and exotic place I know—and yet I regard it as mysteriously homelike: it is a Lübeck translated into oriental fantasy. [5] I maintain that there are altogether remarkable relationships between the two cities which have not been sufficiently investigated. For example, marzipan—which quite obviously means Marci panis, the bread of St. Mark, and thus comes from Venice, furthermore, from the Orient, of course, since it is a typical harem dainty: almonds and rose water!

What you read of mine in the *Morgen* [6] is a fragment of a larger "essay on the theater" which appeared a number of years ago in *Nord und Süd* [7] and contains all sorts of bold, if not impudent assertions (à la marzipan) advocated with great verve. There were a few good things in it, but on the whole I had a stupendous hangover afterward—as always when I have "literated," that is, spoken directly instead of letting things and characters speak.[8] I hope that I shall not have the same experience, to a heightened and unprecedented degree, after my new "Thoughts in War."

Nietzsche—since the beginning of the war I have leafed through him a great deal, though not read him systematically, and especially where he talks about nations, fatherlands,[9] Germany, and imperialism. Here we find enormities spoken. And it becomes ever clearer to me that his hatred of the "Reich" is not directed against German power as such, but against the politicalization, dehumanization, *democratization* of Germany, which has been the *almost* inevitable consequence and concomitant of the seizure of power. It is a dilemma—or is today no longer even that. A man of destiny placed Germany "in the saddle"; she will know how to ride,[10] he said. And she can ride because she must, for she dare not fall off. But it is a ride that probably is leading ever deeper into de-Germanization and ordinariness.

I prefer the *Frankfurter Zeitung* to the *Berliner Tageblatt;* the former strikes me as more substantial and more cultivated without being overdressed. But Theodor Wolff [11] is certainly an excellent journalist, altogether of the Parisian school. I can imagine how amusingly he must write against annexations—after all, he is wholly in favor of "Interior Policy" and at bottom full of scorn for the war. In his editorials nowadays there are sentences like: "There is then no hope that these heroic times will soon end." Quite charming. But in all earnestness, the times are really heroic after all [12] and scorn for them smacks to me too much of cheap scribblers. "The only moral way is to be concerned with what lies within." All very well, but what is at stake here is after all the inner life, the profoundest inner life of nations, and the war is a struggle of one inner life against another, rather than a conflict of outer things against outer things. That, at least, is the way I see it, that is the way I feel it, that is the way I participate in it.

All best wishes and regards!
Yours,
THOMAS MANN.

⊰ 14 ⊱

Tölz
May 8, 1916

Dear Professor:

A letter [1] has obviously been lost—unless you have since received it. In any case I shall briefly recapitulate: Your manuscript was *rejected* in Berlin, with the most favorable comments upon you, on grounds of space and the times; at the same time the editors expressed the hope that they would soon receive something else of yours. I thereupon handed it in to the *Neuer Merkur* (Georg Müller Verlag, Munich), the magazine in which my Frederick essay was first published. I have so far received

only the temporary word that the editor is away on a trip
—that was already some time ago. As soon as I am back in
Munich again—in the middle of this month—I shall telephone to complain.

No more for today; I am deep in work.

Yours, All the best!

THOMAS MANN.

⊶[15]⊷

Munich
June 27, 1916

Dear, dear Professor:

I beg you, do not berate me! Do not come down
hard on me! I am indescribably busy and a miserable correspondent at the present time. My *Betrachtungen eines
Unpolitischen* (originally the essay I had announced for
the *Rundschau* [1]) is growing under my hands to a small
book, which I must labor at to have it done by the autumn. I cannot tell you how much good it does me to talk
all that out, to clarify and have done with what has ir-
ritated and intrigued me for so long. I shall be able afterward to approach my creative tasks with an altogether
new freedom and serenity, I shall also be a better letter-
writer again.

If only I might at least give you some news about your
Rolland today! But the present head of the *Merkur* [2] is a
very amiable gentleman, an Austrian—I beg your pardon; he took the MS home with him some two months

ago, but hasn't read it yet, if you please. I would take it away from him, but then where should it go? It reminds me of a Pole I once saw at the "White Stag" in Dresden, who was so fat that he could not fit into any bathtub: a comparison of whose inappositeness I am fully aware.

Your last fine and stimulating letter, as well as the one before that, still lies on my desk at my right hand. I shall come back to it. Today I only thank you cordially and wish you good fortune and health.

Yours,
THOMAS MANN.

The war is the maddest thing that has ever been: the end more out of sight than ever before. It cannot be decided militarily, but also cannot be decided any other way, so it seems.

◄[16]►

Tölz
September 5, 1916

Dear Professor:

The long interruption in our correspondence, for which I am to blame, has made me thoroughly dissatisfied with myself, or else my general dissatisfaction has been intensified by that. I have not had the summer I would have wished myself. My nerves gave out; there was a crisis after which I had to stay away from my desk altogether for some time; and my recovery to a tolerably productive condition has been a slow process. I was greatly troubled because as the result of this breakdown my main work could not be pushed forward to the degree I had hoped, and that its urgency calls for. I have made some progress, certainly; but there remains far too much still to do— *une mer à boire.* There is a chapter on my indebtedness to three great Germans, Schopenhauer, Nietzsche, and Wagner,[1] which will give you pleasure, I think. In the fall I intend to read it aloud in Munich to a small public circle. At the moment I am wrestling with Rolland [2]— very reverently, as is only right, although he—or perhaps precisely because he (in his war book) did not refrain from using such language as "monstrueux," "démence," "délire d'orgueil," "surenchère criminelle de violence" etc. against me [3] . . . But the name of Rolland brings me to *your* affair, with which I might better have begun.

Yesterday the editor of the *Neuer Merkur* [4] came to the house and I was able to talk with him about your manuscript, which he has read and, moreover, read with great enthusiasm, as I had expected. The size of it would naturally have caused difficulties in any case, but these perhaps could have been overcome. The crucial factor is that the *Merkur* is temporarily shutting up shop; possibly it will later be resumed by another publisher, but for the present the magazine will no longer appear.[5] Evidently things are going ill for Georg Müller Verlag in Munich. The publishing house itself is taking on various gigantic projects (a large *Polish* series [6] has just been announced); but apparently it does not like paying out large sums, and has probably been having to subsidize the *Merkur.* I have therefore requested Dr. Mayer (August), who has been in charge of the editorial department up

73

to the present (he is actually a *Privatdozent* at the Vienna Academy) to send the manuscript to you in Vienna. I hope that before long I shall again be seeing, in another garb and together with more such excellent work,⁷ this fine essay which has had so extraordinarily stimulating an effect upon me.

I do not dare to talk of political matters because I do not know whether it is permissible. There would be a great deal to say and to ask—far more to ask than to say, however. The whole thing is a monstrous question mark painted in blood, to which no man knows any answers.

It is not out of the question that I may be coming to Vienna in the course of the winter. The Urania has invited me, but the matter of fee has not yet been settled.

Until the 15th of this month I shall be staying here; then we must go back to Munich, because of the children's schooling. The winter will not be an easy time— that is already apparent.

All good wishes, dear Professor!

Yours,

Thomas Mann.

◄[17]►

Munich

October 8, 1916

Dear Professor:

Cordial thanks for your friendly furlough letter from Vienna. It is a kind of holiday today; at any rate, flags are waving. They are celebrating the result of the new war bond drive: 10½ billions. The advertising campaign this time was almost on the English or American scale, and it is hard to see how they can go beyond it for the sixth. Indeed, I do not know whether it is really money, but the fiction seems to suffice everywhere nowadays, and if later on it no longer suffices, Germany will squeeze through somehow. The British ministers are saying: "Germany is already ruined and knows it." I have not the slightest proof to the contrary, but my feeling is that Germany will recover swiftest of all, psychically and materially. This feeling is nothing but a symptom—silly testimony of how firm the belief in Germany is in everyone who breathes her air—in spite of highly dubious circumstances and the liveliest wrangling and messes *intra muros*.

I am wondering whether the Rolland manuscript of fond memory reached you while you were still in Vienna. I do hope so, and at any rate made a point of frequently reminding the editors. So the furlough was only an incomplete and nervous pleasure? That will not keep you from looking forward fervently to the next one. If only it proves to be unnecessary! If only a rational peace comes about beforehand! It is for people like you that it is most to be wished for, although we cripples too—I have lost ten pounds, and that is not entirely due to food shortages. Will salvation again come from the East, as at the end of the seven years? I don't know whether one may speak to you of the "separate peace," so much whispered about these days. I almost assume that you would agree, and I should certainly say a fervent Amen.

Aha, so you have discovered Herr Trebitsch's

pamphlet.[1] I call that a find. The comparison you draw between it and your first letter to me is bold, I must confess; I should not have thought of that. For seldom did anything strike me as more intelligent than your letter, and very seldom anything more stupid than Herr Trebitsch's pamphlet. He rightly refers to personal relationships; he has visited me, and since I was a straw widower at the time, I even went out to a restaurant with him once. On the strength of all this, he sent me his essay, to which I could only reply that I had been misunderstood, that apparently his deeply serious nature was not receptive to my mode of expression.[2] With that our personal relations have no doubt come to an early termination, for the manner in which he made use of them in his essay was really not pleasant.[3]

So you have read *Royal Highness* again? Is it really possible? I naturally have a horror to taking up my old things again; but I was recently reflecting on the striking contrast between my second novel and my first.[4] Would anyone believe they were both by the same author? *Buddenbrooks*—growth, burgeoning, luxuriant life; R. H.— a tour de force, calculated, rational, transparent, dominated by an idea which stamps every part, which has something of the conceit about it. Formally speaking "Renaissance," not "Gothic," French, not German; but still very German inwardly, in its feeling for solitude and duty. "Reformation wrapped in Renaissance," a young half-French *homme de lettres* from Mühlhausen wrote me recently. "That is what we are given—and finally a Protestant's journey to Venice." The Fontanesque intonation of Ditlinde even struck me while I was writing.

I am continuing to write away at my *Reflections.*
You will find a sizable sample of them in the January
issue of the *Neue Rundschau.*[5] Before that, in the November issue, another essay, improvised on the occasion
of a new edition of Eichendorff's *Taugenichts* and uncommonly anti-political, is due to appear.[6] That one is
certain to give plenty of offense. But still better is the
fragment in the December issue.[7]

The Vienna lecture is off. I would scarcely be com-
pensated for my expenses. But here in Munich I have
recently given a public reading again: from the early
chapters of the memoirs of the confidence man. The experience gave me fresh ambition to go back to this strange
undertaking and finish it, some time later on. If only my
strength holds out. I must regain those ten pounds—and
am in general quite curious about the surge of gluttony
that will begin in Germany after the end of the blockade.

All best wishes, dear Professor!

Yours,

THOMAS MANN.

◦❁[18]❁◦

Poschinger Strasse 1
Munich
November 25, 1916

Dear Dr. Amann:

An absence of a week, a stay in Berlin where I read
aloud at the "Sezession" and the "Deutsche Gesellschaft,"

sufficed to put me so hopelessly behind in my correspondence and under such pressure that I almost despaired of ever getting things in order again. The greater part of this correspondence is not very interesting or of value to me, but I have long been used to attending to it, both conscientiously and considerately, as part of my duties as a public person. In addition I had quickly to finish something for the January issue of the *Neue Rundschau;* [1] furthermore, there were social demands. In short, at times, though not often, I am really what is called a harried man, and must ask for forbearance—as now for my having made you wait so unconscionably long to thank you for your last letter and accompanying manuscript.

I have read your fine, keen essay with the greatest pleasure—it is altogether worthy of the author of the Rolland study. Since the *Rundschau,* as I happen to know, is glutted and scarcely open to new material, I have again sent the manuscript to the *Frankfurter Zeitung* and feel sure that it will be gratefully accepted there.[2]

It is a melancholy truth, what you say about German eccentricity and inner instability as being the reason for our culture's lack of proselytizing appeal. You do not seem as yet to have given up the hope that this can ever change. I have almost reached that point. I have virtually ceased to believe in "politicalization"—for one reason, I suppose, because at the bottom of my heart I cannot even wish for it. I do not know whether you have seen the November issue of the *Rundschau* with my *Taugenichts* article [3] in which I protest against the "politicalization of culture" advocated by the politicians of literature. I myself have been a stumbling block—although I took a posi-

78

tive stand on this German breakthrough war. I hate democracy and so I hate politics, for it is the same thing. I also hate the jargon of Freemasonry and Jacobinism, which seeks to become the language of the era . . . To literarize, radicalize, politicalize, and Westernize Germany means to de-Germanize her. I am resigned to that, but I won't contribute to it. For it would mean to deprive her of what is weightiest and best about her, her ambiguity—which is, and will remain, a tragic ambiguity.[4] We are no nation like others. Rather, we are something like a Europe in the extract. In our soul, in fact in the soul of the individual German, the contradictions of Europe are fought out.[5] There is no such thing as a national German solidarity and synthesis—or if there is, it exists at most in music, which is our native land, but never, never in culture and in politics. For which reason it is an insane and unnational undertaking to attempt to replace the musical atmosphere of Germany by a literary-political one, as the civilization literati want to do. We are not a nation. For us nationalism [6] is spiritually possible only when we have been trampled into the mud, when everything is going very badly (this war should have gone either very well or very badly; the halfway situation, the security of the Reich's territory coexistent with lack of victory, brings with it extreme moral disintegration). Otherwise it is not possible. The spirit of rising to a challenge, the nation's sense of its own mission, was very strong at the beginning of the war; that feeling lasted only six weeks. Today there is neither pride, nor dignity, nor hatred. There is admiration of the enemy and self-sacrifice and egoistic corruption: *chacun pour soi* and *sauve qui peut.* It looks repellent. We will never amount to anything . . .

But letter paper is not the right medium for these things. This is not a subject which can be put in a nutshell, as the phrase is. Allow me to break off here—since I should never have begun.

Please give my cordial regards to Dr. Strauss [7] and thank him on my behalf for his kind letter. I hope to return to it, but should only like to let him know meanwhile that I was truly delighted.

All good wishes, dear Professor Amann. I assume you will hear directly from the *Frankfurter Zeitung.*

Sincerely yours,

THOMAS MANN.

◄[19]►

Poschinger Strasse 1

Munich

December 16, 1916

Dear Professor:

I want to wish you in good time as good and merry a Christmas as circumstances permit, and at the same time to thank you for your letter of the third—although I cannot really reply to it now. It includes, in addition to friendly agreement, such weighty objections to my comments on *Taugenichts* [1] that a letter is not the proper framework in which I can offer even some degree of defense. I must refer myself and you to my book of confessions, which contains a long chapter on this subject.[2] What is characteristically German, being at once Protestant-Christian and to my mind bourgeois-intellectual, is the refusal to shift the supra-individual into the social; it is the separation of "philosophy" from "politics," i.e. the separation of metaphysical from social life. The great Germans who were the shapers of my nature [3] all adhered to that separation: Schopenhauer most decidedly of all; Wagner in spite of '48—he hated politics: "A political man is repulsive" was one of his sayings; [4] and above all Nietzsche, too, who with profound accuracy called himself the "last unpolitical German." [5] I cannot allow the names you cite to confound me. After all, what did Storm's feeling for liberty and country have to do with modern radical and literary politics,[6] with the politics of the "civilization literati" and their bias toward a civilizational and intellectual homogeneity of "humanity"! . . . I called that separation "Protestant." Recently I read a statement of Hegel's to the effect that France would never come to rest because she had not had the *Reformation.*[7] In other words: we can never settle the problem of political freedom if we do not see it deep beneath metaphysical freedom. Carlyle treats of that, after his fashion, in Volume I of his *Frederick,* the complete German edition of which I discuss in the Christmas issue of the *Frankfurter Zeitung.*[8] . . . *

I must order a halt to this too fluent pen! For the present nothing will be appearing in the *Rundschau.* The chapter in question [9] proved to be improper for political reasons—for appearance in the representative January

* Two pages of the letter omitted here; cf. Introduction, p. 29.

issue, at any rate—and has been postponed. It is too "European"—I can imagine the sardonic face you will make on hearing that. On the other hand, for Christmas the piece I have mentioned is appearing in the *Frankfurter Zeitung,* and then something on music in the red *Tag.*[10]

Perhaps we shall return to the matter of the "Academy" [11] after the war—How do you like the peace offer? [12] At least it is very complicatedly German: disingenuous and cunning.

Cordially yours,
THOMAS MANN.

◄[20]►

Munich
January 31, 1917

Dear Professor:

I have just this moment received your letter and hasten to tell you how much it would delight me to greet you here in the flesh. Beginning of March? It is not absolutely certain that I shall be here then, for imagine, Berlin wishes, and the ambassador in *Stockholm* also wishes, that I deliver a lecture there, an assignment I can scarcely withdraw honorably from, since it has come to me. The settling of a date presents difficulties. I cannot go right away, for I must have time to work out a lecture, which for this special purpose would have to be done in all deliberation. But who can know what the world will look like in eight, six, or even only four or five weeks?

Well, I have left it to the ambassador's discretion to undertake the first steps in the negotiations in any case, and will then see what I can decide with the Swedish organization which is arranging the affair. I should imagine the adventure itself would take up ten days to two weeks. I can only hope that these will not fall during the time of your furlough! For I am looking forward eagerly to meeting you personally, and am confident that we shall get on well with one another, in spite of inhibitions on both sides.

I was thoroughly annoyed with the *Frankfurter Zeitung* that time.[1] The rejection itself was a mistake, the reason given downright foolish. Ordinarily I think highly of the sheet, but this has greatly alienated me from it.

May I wait until I can hand the *Animal mirabile* [2] to you personally? For I *have* it—and should like to keep it a while; on first reading of the manuscript my impressions were so strange and somewhat confused that I should like to take it up again and come to a clearer view. It is a remarkable and attractive production, as far as I can tell.

I forgot to ask you to say nothing to anyone, for the present, about this projected trip to Sweden.

Let us *hope,* then, for the beginning of March, dear Professor. It would be a real pleasure to me.

Yours,

THOMAS MANN.

◄[21]►

Poschinger Strasse 1 (Last
house on Föhringer Allee,
entrance from the Allee!)
Munich
March 3, 1917
Dear Professor:
I shall *certainly* be here, have heard nothing from
Stockholm and would not at all feel like going at present.
So come! My wife and I are awaiting you with pleasure.
Only let us know—a telephone call immediately upon
your arrival in the city will suffice. We can then make
arrangements. Have a good trip. Until we meet!
Yours,
T.M.

◄[22]►

Munich
March 25, 1917
Dear Professor:
That you cannot come is certainly a disappointment
to me, but scarcely a surprise: the military situation led
me to expect that furloughs would continue to be canceled. Your reticent hints of *your* disappointment, your
grief at these years of unnatural separation from the real
basis of your life, moved me deeply—and yet that is only

the negative side of what you are bearing, enduring, accomplishing, sacrificing, you and millions of others. Almost every letter with a military postmark makes me ashamed of my sitting by the hearth, my "leisure hours." "To suffer with you was a gain . . ." Etc.[1] But everyone has his role, his "character," and no one is entitled to believe that he could wish himself different—in hindsight. As a Schopenhauerian I am convinced of the metaphysical freedom of the will—and its empirical unfreedom.

The "situation" is certainly more depressing than ever. I can sympathize with the envious amazement of the Allied press at the absolute confidence, indeed the pride, with which the German people accepts our "strategic retreat" in the West [2]—it is certainly also quite a philosophical problem whether this is a matter of free or unfree will. . . . *

I find the Russian business [3] enough to make one stand on one's head—including the way the French are rejoicing over it. Hervé's,[4] for example, with his, "One might go mad with joy!" Is a popular government such as is now being advocated in Germany at all possible in Russia? Is even mere "democracy" in the bourgeois sense possible there? There is no bourgeoisie, after all! I wonder what Dostoevsky would have thought and said to all this. I am occupying myself a good deal now with his political and literary writings, his type of conservatism, his position on the Slavophile and Western movements, on "nihilism," as that position is expressed in, say, the Pushkin address.[5] It is extremely interesting to me in reference to my own intellectual and political position

* One sentence omitted: cf. Introduction, p. 29.

between nationalism and "nihilism"—I mean, between Germanism and Europeanism. An ambiguous position strange to the point of weirdness, to the point of sheer irony toward both sides. This constitutes the basic theme of my by now boundless literary work—also of the chapter from it which has appeared in the March issue of the *Rundschau*.⁶ I cannot send it to you because the *Rundschau* ignores the institution of offprints, but should like to call your attention to it, if only on account of what is said there about "Nietzsche as educator." The book is *une mer à boire*,⁷ and every other moment I tingle with impatience to be free to tell stories again, to engage in unhampered art. I am wasting these years almost as I would had I been conscripted.⁸ I shall certainly be still occupied with this thing until late in the summer, and then I shall again have put myself between two stools—with a degree of grace, I hope.

Is peace really in sight now? Russia's "internal policy" seems after all to be determined by her foreign policy for the present, that is, by the determination to win the war. And I have never shared the excessive enthusiasm for the undersea boats, in so far as it was excessive. But I hear experts declare with assurance that England really cannot hold out longer than August. If only that were so! Peace of course would instantly mean an enormous relief and spiritual release. But then what happens inside the country would count! I consider even something like a civil war not out of the question; thought so even before the Russian Revolution. In any case we shall never again be free of politics, and the newspapers will no doubt go on appearing with big headlines to the end of our lives. A pretty prospect. But oddly enough, politics and in fact the political problems of the war remain in my blood and mind, as they did even before this war in whose coming I did not believe. The novel, in the midst of which I was interrupted,[9] had a pedagogico-political main theme: a young man was placed between a Latin oratorical advocate of "labor and progress," a disciple of Carducci [10]—and a despairingly witty reactionary —in Davos where an unvirtuous sympathy with death [11] holds him fast . . . Do you see? And I had to write these *Betrachtungen* only because otherwise the novel, as a result of the war, would have been unbearably overburdened intellectually.[12]

You are reading *Buddenbrooks* again? I will not conceal my delight in learning that. I have been told the same thing from various quarters of late, and in fact during the war the book has had no fewer than fifteen new editions. The hundredth is slowly approaching; [13] and say what you will, the reason must be somewhat different than for the scores of other books of the past several decades. Recently a mama sent me the composition notebook of her sixteen-year-old daughter in which the child had treated *Buddenbrooks* under the heading of "What is my favorite book and why," or something of the sort. Strange [14] to think that this child lay in her cradle while I was writing the book, that she grew up into life along with the book, she and others. In the letters that come to me a particular turn of phrase occurs repeatedly: that with my things I have "helped them to live." Well, I did not start out with any such benevolent social concept in mind; that I freely admit; I had too many problems with

87

myself to conceitedly imagine that I would be able to help others. And yet I have helped others, and quite obviously *many* others, to live! I was not being social, not political; I did not pose with my right hand on my heart and my left in the air, reciting the *Contrat social.*[15] And therefore I was no "fighter," but an "aesthete." [16] And still I helped people to live. That much I may tell myself at forty, and if I accomplish no more to the day of my death, I shall also be able to say it still in death.

It is tasteless to the point of being offensive that I talk so much about myself. But never before have I been so compelled to reflect upon myself as I have been these past years. The need of the nation is also my personal need—that may well be the only reason I have so linked myself to it, to the ire and scorn of the anti-nationalists.

In my remark about the two novels [17] I was being your pupil. "In depicting a character or an event the French imagination orients itself by an idea, an intellectual formula, which only then is narrowed down by a more or less precise description, i.e. material definition, and is finally approximated to that impression of uniqueness which engenders the illusion of life. . . . This intellectual domination does not permit the creative shaping of pure spontaneity, which is to say, the maximum intensity of life . . ." That is from your Rolland study, if you will recall, and it is the precise definition of *Royal Highness,* whereas *Buddenbrooks* represents the precise opposite of that.

What is in the offing? The offensive against Gabriele's [18] hosts? War of movement in the West? Then the Westerners will be defeated! And you, will you be coming under fire? Had I, poor skeptic, any right to such phrases, I would gladly say: God protect you!

In any case accept my best wishes and regards.

Yours,

T.M.

⊲[23]⊳

Munich
April 16, 1917

Dear Professor:

There's a pretty mess! Exactly what the word "pretty" implies, namely unfortunate, derisive, jinxed, and embarrassing. And I have reproaches to make against myself. I could not believe my ears yesterday when upon my return my wife informed me what had happened; and she in turn had not believed hers when the girl told her that a Herr Amann had called and was very sorry not to find me in! On the 31st you write to me: in two weeks. And said that a card would precede your telephone call. An old acquaintance was staying in Mittenwald on the Tyrolian border, and asked me there. I felt worn and bored by work, and so I went for a few days. That was on Tuesday. I suppose it was thoughtless, but after all I knew that I could be back in four hours, if your card came. It did not. I had counted on remaining until Friday or Saturday, had fairly good luck with the weather, and stayed until Sunday. Sunday afternoon I was back here, and the malheur had already happened. I cannot acquit myself of a venial sin. I should have left a message for you, just in case. But now what about you! We must also draw up the countercharges. You were very sorry, you said, and therewith your voice withdraws and no one can lay hands on you. No hotel address, no word about the length of your stay—which after all probably could have been prolonged another twelve hours. My wife, if she had had anything to go by, would have captured you: a telephone call to Mittenwald and I would have hastened back in forced marches. In short, an altogether muddled affair. To think that you came to Munich chiefly, if not specially, so that we could meet. What now? Are you furious? I am. Or, if not furious, at any rate disappointed and reproachful toward myself and you. I am writing to Vienna where you have "conceivably" gone from here. No, if you were furious, you are so no longer, since you must now be with your family. Instead of concerning myself with the question of what route you will have been contemplating for your return to the front, I should probably do better to think of the peace—which now must come one way or another; at least that is what the voice of the people is proclaiming with assurance. Though since the American democracy is preparing for three years of war, we must place our hopes in the Russian democracy. And if everything goes to pieces, it will be the German democracy's turn.

Refresh yourself with home and native soil, and think without bitterness of

Yours,
THOMAS MANN.

◄[24]►

Munich
April 21, 1917
Dear Professor:
Forgive me for having forgotten to mention the two
manuscripts in my recent letter. The Cellini [1] is no less
fine than the *Animal*, but since the *Frankfurter Zeitung*
behaved so badly last time,[2] I do not quite know where
to send it. The *Berliner Tageblatt?* You ought to try it.
And by all means say that I suggested that you do so . . .
No, let me see, it occurs to me that the features editor
of the Munich *Neueste Nachrichten* is an old acquaintance of mine.[3] That might work out. I shall therefore
keep this manuscript and hope soon to be able to send it
to you printed. And after the war we'll do the essay volume [4]—*without* your paying the printing costs. That
wouldn't do!

With best regards,
Yours,
THOMAS MANN.

◄[25]►

Munich
June 30, 1917
Dear Professor:
I trust you have meanwhile received the letter [1] in
which I replied to your news from Agram. Its content was

in essence: "Thank God that it has turned out this way!" [2] And that came from the heart. Home nursing, furlough, leisure, opportunity to work—that is really wonderful. I am happy to share in the success which you are already having before the publication of the *Animal. Rundschau?* possibly. But I do not really "see" it there. It would look a good deal handsomer, I think, in a large feature section. Since you have made his acquaintance, would you not like to try Dr. Martens [3] once more, who is ambitious to publish good things?

I am working like a horse in order to finish my present endless declaration and interminable lamentation by fall.[4] I am in the midst of a chapter on Virtue.[5] Then comes one on Humaneness. Then one on Belief which is thoroughly unbelieving.[6] Then one on Aestheticistic Politics. Then one on Radicalism. Then one on Irony and Conservatism.[7] And then it will be, I think, complete. But even before there is discussion of a thousand and one things. I think it will be the strangest of all literary products of the war.

I am going to Tölz on July 15, although I do not know whether I shall have anything to eat there. I shun traveling, and am also "indispensable" at home. But if you were to come some time, that would be splendid. We must get out of the habit of waiting for the peace. All in all, this is no "war," but rather some inchoate upheaval for which no name has yet been found. But just as during the Fr. Revolution, life meanwhile goes its way for the noncombatants (insofar as anyone is a noncombatant). Even the life of art: We recently had here a "Pfitzner Week" arranged by Walter, and the première of *Pales-*

trina [8]—a work with which I instantly became wildly in-
fatuated (I had scarcely thought that would ever happen
to me again). I know why, too. It [9] is a piece of dying
Romanticism, a kind of final product of the Wagner-
Schopenhauerian spirit, something absolutely enchanting
for me in its metaphysical mood, its archaic-hieratic
stylization, its profound melancholy, its ethos of "cross,
death, and the tomb," [10] and its humor! Its appearance at
this moment was for me no more and no less than a great
piece of good fortune; it made me affirmative, released
me from polemicism, and it has offered to my emotional
life a great object to which it can cling, and from the
viewpoint of which all that is repugnant is revealed as
flimsy appearance . . .[11] But I am no doubt raving in-
comprehensibly. The best of luck! I wish your wounds
healing, your mind composure and serenity—in the consciousness of duty so magnificently done.

Yours,
THOMAS MANN.

◄[26]►

Tölz
July 29, 1917

Dear Professor:

I very, very well understand your wish; [1] moreover,
I share it with all my heart. You know how I prize the
pieces, and especially the two principal ones, the studies on
Rolland and Fontane. I am therefore ready at any mo-

ment, and with real eagerness, to aid you to the limit of my abilities. I have thought of Georg Müller and of Albert Langen, especially of the latter firm, for I am well acquainted with the director.[2] But I cannot and would not wish to conceal from you my doubts whether we will achieve anything at the present moment. Quite candidly, I do not have much hope; the times are unfavorable. In the first place there is a shortage of paper; my own publisher complains about this constantly and says that this is why the projected popular-priced new edition of *Royal Highness* has not yet been brought out. Furthermore, in keeping with your Romance sympathies, the book treats exclusively French subjects: Rolland, the French element in Fontane, the French national character (also not exactly viewed in a wartime light, I should think); and however you may choose to call such censorship un-German or see in it an underestimation of the public, my feeling is that no publisher will ask readers to swallow anything of the sort right now. Even Bie,[3] who undoubtedly thought very highly of the Rolland essay, refused it because he considered *now* was not the moment for it. In addition there is the season: the holidays, people are away. I do not know, but I think that Holm, too, the manager of Langen, is also not in Munich. Would it not be better to wait until autumn, if not until peacetime, in the hope that possibly the two may coincide? But that is only a question—and I myself will not give an affirmative answer if your altogether justified impatience answers no. In that case I suggest that we make a start with Albert Langen Verlag, Hubertusstrasse, Munich. Send the manuscript there, and as soon as you inform me that it is on its way I shall write to Holm, and really put my shoulder to the wheel, you can be sure of that.

Yours,

THOMAS MANN.

·❧ 27 ❧·

Bad Tölz
August 27, 1917

Dear Professor:

Your furlough must be drawing to an end—and I do not want you to be going out once again without a greeting, a token of my friendly regard. This letter aims to be no more; evidently I shall only be able to write decent letters again once I am free of the morning scribbling and again making "music." Until then the revulsion I have against taking up my pen in the afternoons is almost insuperable.

Here in the country, too, I have been doing my best to move this monstrosity along. I shall be staying here until the middle of September. October, November . . . then it will and must be finished, and I think then that with many a head-shaking I shall set as a motto to it: "*Mais que diable allait-il faire dans cette galère?*" [1]

Perhaps it will be nice to travel then; strikingly enough, in this of all years I have received a number of invitations for lectures and at the moment am engaged in putting together a "tournée." It will be a huge zigzag: Essen-Ruhr—Posen, Bromberg, Elbing, Königsberg, Danzig, Oldenburg, and Bremen. Strenuous, but in part interesting and fairly lucrative.

Have I already written to you about the profound impression that Hans Pfitzner's *Palestrina* in the Munich Prinzregenten Theater made upon me? [2] A fabulously German, singular, autocratic, and thoughtful work, a late and ultimate product of the Wagnerian-Schopenhauerian, the Romantic realm, which, you know, is really the homeland of my psychic life. The experience fitted almost miraculously into the framework of my book,[3] and I have given the pages I wrote about it to the *Rundschau* for prior publication there.[4]

You, too, have been telling me about pleasures in the theater. My brother's play (a Berlin humor sheet called it *Mme Engros* [5] because of the length of the run) is unquestionably a powerful throw of the dice. Its counterpart would be, say, a drama on Luther performed today in Paris. How would that be greeted? Which is not meant to say anything against the French.

You have touched a sore point there, dear Professor. The relationship between my brother and myself, delicate for years, was no longer tenable after the outbreak of the war. I would gladly have kept it going a while longer, come what may and cost what it might; but my brother's political passion is stronger than his human feelings; he despises Germany, or at any rate the Germany of this war, too intensely to have forborne branding my attitude as a crime against justice and truth and making the break. A painful and shameful affair.[6] I gladly do him the honor of believing that he too suffers on its account. . . .*

Accept, then, my cordial wishes for your welfare! Keep me informed about your address, your experiences!

Yours,

THOMAS MANN.

⊰[28]⊱

Munich

March 2, 1918

Dear Professor:

It was a pleasure to me to hear from you again. I for my part did not write in the first place because I was no longer sure of your address, but then also simply out of *gêne:* I no longer want to show my face even in writing until my "book" is out at last—though whether I shall be able to show my face afterward is another question. I have been finished for the past several weeks;[1] the monstrosity is concluded: twelve chapters, politics, morality, art, philosophy, autobiography, an indescribable ragout, a thing without genre, quite without precedent. The human elements in it will win you over to it about halfway; otherwise I could not count upon your sympathy. I am writing away at a preface now which will sum up the motifs of the whole in the manner of a musical prelude, and am meanwhile intriguing with officialdom (with the aid of, as the phrase is nowadays, an "understanding" ministerial councilor) in order to

* Two sentences omitted; cf. Introduction, p. 29.

obtain an extra ten tons of printing paper for my publisher. For there is a great scarcity of that.

You are in safety, you can live—that is the main thing to *me*. And do you not also think that peace is on the way? But what do you say to "democracy," what do you say to the bourgeois rhetoricians of the dear West, who do not want to end the war, which after the victory of Germany [2] (in the broadest sense) is nothing but an atrocious bane—who want to keep it up at the open risk of plunging Europe into anarchistic revolution? You know my hobbyhorse, my hatred; it is the rhetorical bourgeois, the politicians, the illuminate and Three-Points-Man,[3] stockholders in a newspaper *qui répand les lumières*.[4] History will demonstrate that they made this war against us . . .

I might tell a great deal about my trip [5] in January: Strassburg (Pfitzner [6]), Essen (Krupp), Brussels (*Fiorenza* in the Théatre du Parc [7]), Rostock (the Duke's court), Lübeck [8] . . . but these cue words must suffice.

I shall scarcely be writing again before I can send you the *Betrachtungen*.

Recently I took up your Fontane study [9] again—I am now reading the old fellow once more, with incredible pleasure. An excellent monograph on him will be appearing soon; author, a Dr. Wandrey.[10] I know the Effi Briest chapter. Altogether the time is ripe for good books. Also one on Nietzsche by my friend Dr. Ernst Bertram [11] is in the offing. And do you know the Conrad Ferdinand Meyer by Baumgarten? [12] The best of luck!

Yours,
Thomas Mann.

◆[29]◆

Poschinger Strasse 1
Munich
May 23, 1918

My dear Professor:
Your card of the 17th arrived punctually today.
Many thanks for it. Have you received the letter which
I dispatched about four weeks ago to your previous ad-
dress? [1]

I am in the midst of correcting proofs on my hereti-
cal book, but alongside that am again engaged in something novelistic, or at least something figurative. [2] I shall
see; it is still going tolerably well.

I am glad to know that you are in safety and not
engaged in too rough occupations.

Yours,
THOMAS MANN.

◆[30]◆

Poschinger Strasse 1
Munich
July 11, 1918

Dear Professor:
I see that in accordance with old habit you addressed your letter of June 28, which I received yesterday, to Tölz. Those are *tempi passati;* the little property

99

there no longer belongs to us; we sold it last year, partly in order to be more mobile in the summers once again and because I should like to take the children to the Baltic Sea; partly also because the cottage was growing too small for us. There were other disadvantages besides. Of course had we known that an increase in our family was impending (six weeks ago I became a father for the fifth time, after an interval of seven years, of a baby daughter [1]) . . . . *—we would naturally have kept Tölz for this year. As it is we have now rented a place on the Tegern Lake, near a village named Abwinkel. It is called Villa Defregger (the owner is the son of a painter and is away fighting) and we shall move there tomorrow, when the holidays begin, for as many weeks as are officially permitted us. For even in respect to freedom of movement there are now all sorts of restrictions; these, like other such measures, will possibly "prove their worth" and be perpetuated . . . I confess that in spite of all I feel a certain awe of what the future will be like, and am beginning to ask myself whether for my kind of person, and the after all loose and unorganized things that my kind of person has to offer, there will be any room in it at all. I have been going over my various projects in order, and have compunctions about each one of them, particularly the Confidence Man; the best-written scene in it so far is where he simulates epileptic symptoms before the draft board.[2] To be sure, its offensiveness is only external, and at bottom he is a militarist—as incidentally all my heroes are. But for the next ten years I shall probably not be able to read aloud from that publicly.

* Several words omitted; cf. Introduction, p. 29.

I am glad that you have read the Baumgarten.[3] It is certainly a fine book. I would call your slight resistance to the revelation of secrets and to psychological indiscretion strikingly *conservative* (for what is more democratic than psychology?). But when you consider that B. is a Budapest Jew (very rich, incidentally, and also an invalid; he has to have a nurse constantly at his side and walks with a cane, a monocle in his eye)—then you must agree that it has come off reasonably well. The *Tonio Kröger* quotation will not have escaped you, in spite of the missing quotation marks. I do not feel their absence as theft, but on the contrary as a homage; the phrase about the *bourgeois manqué* and the artist with a guilty conscience seems altogether to have "sunk in," and no longer to need quotes, let alone reference to the source.[4]

I have been reading a great deal of Stifter lately and am taking a volume of the "Studies" to the country with me. That is a discovery to which I have come, matured, late. But then how short a time it is since I began to understand anything about Goethe's prose. The Stifter atmosphere is enormously to my liking. It is still pre-bourgeois and yet is what I call bourgeois in the highest sense, most beautifully expressed in his statement that his works are not merely works of art, but ethical revelations, stringently conserved human dignity.[5] Perhaps that is what has won me over as a member of his reading public . . .

My "book" will scarcely be published before September. The page proofs are being held up at the moment; the question is whether it is to be one or two volumes. I am for its coming out in one volume, in spite of the

650 pages.[6] It is a *malheur* of accumulated brooding, and ought to look that way. But the publisher has practical objections.

One must spend a great deal of money on food; then one can manage. I nourish myself chiefly on honey, which is my favorite food anyhow, although I am not a bear in other respects; and my wife has hoarded an ample supply of it.

Yours,
THOMAS MANN.

◄[31]►

Schiedhalden Strasse 33
Küsnacht-Zürich
February 7, 1935

My very dear Herr Dr. Amann:

Many thanks for your letter, this benign resumption of relations, which has gladdened but not surprised me, because I always considered you a person of high principle. Indeed, I have occasionally wondered, when I heard or read about you, that you did not come sooner, and I tell myself now that probably a happier situation, the enhancement of your reputation, the serenity of success,[1] was necessary to give you the inner freedom to do so.

I have never held any grudge against you, and have sincerely regretted the misunderstanding that came between us. The book which you attacked,[2] that "last great rear-guard action of the romantic middle-class mentality in the face of advancing 'modernity,' an action conducted not without gallantry," as I once called it,[3] had its legitimate place in my life and in the times; since I freed myself from its attitudes in good time, I have no regrets. That it would displease you, I had to take into the bargain, and I did so all the more readily since the motives of your embitterment were obviously love and reverence —for R. Rolland, of whom I had spoken deprecatingly and whom, for all my respect, I have never really learned to love—any more than he has me. In short, the thing was grievous to me, but understandable, and I could only pass over it to the next items on the agenda, which were becoming ever more demanding.

It is a curious coincidence that your letter from Athens was waiting for me here when I returned from Vienna, which I had not seen for three years and where I have just spent a few days rich in pleasant experiences. In spite of a certain down-at-heels quality, it remains an enchanting, gypsylike, and artistic city, and I might be strongly tempted to carry out the works of my old age there. My infatuation with it is not surprising . . . .* and the words of persuasion I heard there, that I ought to move after all, continue to ring in my ears. But I suppose one does well to look on for a while . . . In any case I consider the spread of fascism inexorable everywhere, in differing phases, of course, and it remains to be proved that Austria will succeed in preserving her peculiar nuance. If that were so, I would probably prefer Vienna to any other point as a residence, and our all-too-

* Several words omitted; cf. Introduction, p. 29.

literary acquaintanceship could become rooted in a personal one that would better withstand new assaults.

With good wishes and regards,
Yours sincerely,
THOMAS MANN.

◄[32]►

Schiedhalden Strasse 33
Küsnacht-Zürich
February 21, 1936

Dear Doctor:

Many, many thanks! You must put up with me: my correspondence has swelled enormously as the result of that brash stunt—it is touching and almost dismaying to me to see how much emotion these few simple and obvious words have aroused [1]—and, moreover, I must see to bringing the third volume of *Joseph* to its conclusion; the last part, the love affair with Potiphar's wife, is a literary adventure in small as the whole work is in large.

You assume rightly: the letter was a pure outburst of temper, unpremeditated, scarcely intended, a venting at last, and no doubt necessary for my spiritual health, of all the aversion and disgust which that scandalous mess arouses daily. And then I let it stand and go its way, trusting that this would be the right hour for it, and also wishing somewhat to stiffen the spine of the "emigration," external and internal; and at the same time to correct certain unpleasant half-and-half ideas that might

104

still be lingering in the world in regard to my relationship to the Third Reich. Naturally I am expecting the beasts who form the German government these days to deprive me of my citizenship [2] and to ban my books. But how long will these edicts be valid? I tell myself: either war will be here in one and a half or two years, or within the same period things in Germany will change so that my books, too, will be possible again. All my countrymen who come to see me here assure me that dissolution has progressed to an unbelievable degree, that the final stage has been reached.

If I can possibly manage, I intend to deliver the festival lecture for Freud's eightieth birthday at the Vienna Academic Society for Medical Psychology,[3] and perhaps also read there in June during the festival weeks. One way or the other, I hope to see you.[4]

Yours sincerely,
THOMAS MANN.

❧[33]❧

Schiedhalden Strasse 33
Küsnacht-Zürich
October 14, 1936

Dear Doctor:

Many thanks for the nice package. By way of reciprocation a flimsy return present, only 752 pages, with a "phenomenon" on the jacket, follows under separate cover.[1] Do not be alarmed; put it away and give yourself time *until* you read it and *when* you read it! The intellectual serenity of your story,[2] charmingly uncontemporary as it is, makes it somewhat easier for me to send you these extended jests, which are sure to be condemned as superfluous and inopportune. Nevertheless they are my way of meeting these last three years head on, in fact of snapping my fingers at them.

At the moment my streak of bad luck is continuing without a break. I had hoped to recuperate by the sea in southern France only to be stricken by an angina; no sooner was I back home than I had an eruption of erysipelas from which I am only slowly recovering; and for the past week I have been bothered by an infected finger on my right hand; it had to be opened, and now, swaddled in bandage, forms a hampering irritation from morning to night—particularly interfering with writing, which is very bad for it, and vice versa also. . . .*

With that, I must take my leave. Once again, thank you for the good, the very good entertainment in violet and black!

Yours sincerely,
Thomas Mann.

* One paragraph omitted; cf. Introduction, page 29.

⊲[34]⊳

Schiedhalden Strasse 33
Küsnacht-Zürich
November 25, 1936

Dear Dr. Amann:

Both your fine and interesting letters, expressions
of thanks themselves, call for thanks in return—you have
given me great pleasure, touched me and also disturbed
me, as I am always disturbed by the thought that sending someone such a book [1] imposes upon the recipient
not only the reading but also the obligation of responding: trouble and work which may ill conform with his
other desires and obligations in regard to work. I can
only hope that the pleasure in my productions really was
great enough so that the sacrifice in time and energy
which expressions of thanks such as yours represent will
not have been felt too strongly as a sacrifice.

The matter of your book [2] has been going around
in my mind since you wrote me about it again: wrote of
the new phase into which it has entered, so to speak.
Only last night we were speaking with our friend E. von
Kahler (he is writing a big book on the German character in the world [3]), and I learned from him that Schocken
Verlag [4] has also been forbidden to continue publishing
the writings of Kafka [5] apparently on the same grounds
as your work: simply because their field extends too far
beyond the Jewish sphere and therefore the ghetto publishing house is exceeding its prescribed limits. It is perfectly evident to me that this was sufficient reason for

the usurpers to ban your book also, and for that reason
perhaps it was a mistake that you gave the work, which
is not at all specialized, to this specialized house. Though,
to be sure, the choice was probably not large; but would
not Reichner or Zsolnay [6] have taken it? What can, what
must be done now? The question preoccupies me, for I
feel very strongly that this good, wise, and helpful book
must be brought out into the world again. I would gladly
try—and certainly shall try—to communicate this feeling to a Swiss publisher, for example Niehans; but have
to overcome the understandable timidity of these busi-
nessmen in regard to books that cannot be imported into
Germany. Toward Niehans in particular, who would
otherwise be the logical person, I have a guilty conscience
because I prevailed on him to publish a book on myself
(by Ferd. Lion) which was promptly banned in Germany.[7] (Do you know that no review of the *Joseph* is
allowed to be published there?) Hermann Hesse [8] himself has told me how intensely he, too, was interested in
your book. He had already spoken to me about it in
Montagnola before I had read it. I must confer with him.
Have you taken soundings anywhere in Vienna yet? I
would be inclined to think of Bermann-Fischer,[9] but do
so only with painful doubts. He absolutely does not want
to be an exiles' publishing house or, although his is a
Jewish firm, to publish exclusively Jews. But still, would
you not care to go to him some time? I would gladly
arrange the *entrevue*.

Having just had word by telephone that Ossietzky
has received the Nobel Peace Prize,[10] I went to St. Gall
yesterday to do a benefit reading for the children of

exiles. Even while I was reading, I was filled with joy over the news. At last a stirring announcement, a sign of courage, of opposition in the world after all the soft-stepping and all the timid retreating. The fury of the regime is unbounded, of course, and I consider it possible that poor Ossietzky, who by now may be completely broken in spirit, may be forced to reject the prize. And what shall we say to the subjugation of the Spanish people (though it has not quite come to that yet) by European fascism? And what about the indignation felt in Berlin, in this instance so deeply justified morally, over the condemnation of the German Stickling in Russia? [11] It seems to me that even at this late date Holland ought to break off diplomatic relations with Germany over van der Lubbe.

Let us let be, little as things ought to be let be. I am writing a novella about Goethe in his old age.[12] Difficult. Thank you for your fine capacity for enjoyment and for praise!

Yours sincerely,
THOMAS MANN.

◄[35]►

Schiedhalden Strasse 33
Küsnacht-Zürich
March 23, 1937

Dear Dr. Amann:

I congratulate you on the manly decision to wend your way homeward again.[1] Never does that question of

Fontane's, "What is the good of it all?"[2] strike us so
closely as it does on journeys. Still, the change of air will
have had its refreshing effects; but you are to be envied
that you have put traveling behind you again and are
back in your proper sphere, while I must arm myself—in
the most literal sense—for the impending journey to the
antipodeans, at the beginning of the coming month, in
order to peddle ideas among them, or in plain language,
to make a fool of myself.[3] A hundred preparations are
needed, learning lectures in English, etc. etc., and it
makes me furious because it is tearing me away for weeks
and weeks from my proper work, which I am burning to
get at. I want to cut the lecture and dinner circuit as
short as possible, and by omitting Holland, where I was
also supposed to throw my literary weight about, be back
here again by the beginning of May.

Your novel [4]—I was actually scarcely able to do
more than look into it. An extremely clever utopia, it
seems to be. I have for the present sent the manuscript
to Lion,[5] who is at the moment working for the magazine
in Paris; he will probably bring it back to me within the
next few days. I am afraid that he will tell me what I
have already told myself: that fragments of novels are
a perilous matter for a periodical. A fine essay in the vein
of *Tradition und Weltkrise,* a book that Editor Lion also
admires enormously, would be far, far better.

Charming, the passage in the letter about Lotte.[6]
It is remarkable how much encouragement that sort of
thing gives, even though it does not really have anything
to do with the matter.

If you have anything to communicate to Lion dur-

ing my absence, it would be best to write him % Oprecht
and Heibling, Publishers, Zürich, Rämistrasse.

Sincerely yours,
THOMAS MANN.

⊸[36]⊷

[no date] [1]

Dear Dr. Amann:

Many thanks for your letter and the manuscript. I
read it at once, with the closest attention. These are remarkable, touching, and grotesque human documents.
I am passing the pages on to Lion, who must decide
whether these things will fit in with us. I wonder
whether the publication of them might not be taken
amiss in France. Moreover it is too bad that some of the
letters [2] have already appeared in German.

Would you also, please, take occasion some time
to let me have a note on Claude Berry! [3] I know nothing
about him, and doubt that Lion does. Furthermore, it is
not clear to me where he obtained the material. Unde-
liverable letters are usually returned to the sender, after
all. How did Berry have the opportunity to examine these
masses of intimate correspondence? I would be grateful
for this information. You will hear further on the matter
from Lion.

Warm greetings from

Your much too busy
THOMAS MANN.

◄[37]►

Schiedhalden Strasse 33
Küsnacht-Zürich
September 13, 1937

Dear Dr. Amann:

You will meanwhile have received the war letters back from Lion. I have had no luck with him on these documents. He has probably explained to you the reasons for the rejection. What it boils down to is that he does not consider the publication of French letters from the World War exactly an urgent matter for our magazine. I must admit that he is not entirely wrong: the audience we count on is certainly looking for something more affirmative and creative from us, and that is what we have promised, after all.

I hope that you have had a good rest in Berg [1] and are now better able to cope with the air of Vienna. I am still rather tired from what I have been through [2] and at the same time overburdened, for in addition to my current work the magazine imposes upon me a great deal of wracking my brains, as well as work in the more immediate sense. Right now I am on the point of going to the Ticino for a few weeks, to Locarno, for the drier air and in order to be getting to bed early for a while. There is little chance of my visiting Vienna this winter. I must keep close at my work these next few months, for by the second half of February, health permitting, I shall have to set out for America again, this time for a regular tour through twelve or fourteen cities, which will extend deep into the West.[3]

> Most cordial greetings and good wishes,
> Sincerely yours,
> THOMAS MANN.

⋅[38]⋅

> 1550 San Remo Drive
> Pacific Palisades, California
> June 26, 1948

Dear Dr. Amann:

My warm thanks for your entertaining "sick visit." [1] It was no longer that, for the malheur lies some three months back, and I can again use the arm almost to a normal degree, although the musculature as a whole is still somewhat sore. I have healed the thing very rapidly. I put this in the active mood because healing is really very vigorous work, in which the whole organism takes part, as I well observed from the fatigue that followed. Breaking a bone is a real shock. When I lay on the floor, I said to myself in utter consternation: "My God!" and immediately had the feeling that something altogether impermissible had happened. I was also chalk-white and had to sit down. Most people lose consciousness.

Certainly the blame lay solely with an agonizing and unbearable transition state between tasks. I found it very difficult to start on something new after the *Faustus.* My life stood, and stands, under the sign of "Never again." And yet, what despairs I endured while writing it! Often enough it appeared a devastating certainty to me that I was obviously and with open eyes spoiling the book. Afterward one believes every word of praise, and tears filled my eyes only at the first ones.

Then I studied Middle High German and have written a good part of a medieval legend, a refashioning in prose of Hartmann von der Aue's *Gregorius auf dem Steine*. I find the man born of incest who then marries his mother and finally becomes Pope so exceedingly comic. You will see to what extent that is still related to *Faustus*. I am interrupting my work on it just now to write an autobiographical fragment on the period during which I was working on *Faustus,* an altogether wild era, 1943–46.[2] The day on which your pupil Goldberg[3] stood in the sea water outside Caën, or wherever it was, comes into it, then my seventieth birthday, then my severe illness (due to the book), and the German collapse.

Now I can no longer go into your remarks on *Tonio Kroeger* and the translation samples, which seemed to me quite elegant. But these efforts move me. Give my regards to the two gentlemen! It is something that this typical little product of youth, my "Werther," and at the same time a curious mixture of Nietzsche and *Immensee,* should go on pleasing young people.

I hope you are living *well,* enjoying your work, are in good health and little affected by the alarming activities within this country—and outside it. *Tradition und Weltkrise* remains palpable to me.

Yours,
THOMAS MANN.

⟨ 39 ⟩

1550 San Remo Drive
Pacific Palisades, California
November 21, 1948

Dear Dr. Amann:

A pleasure, your letter. How good to hear your sensible voice again, especially on *Faustus,* which in this inexperienced country naturally encounters a great deal of indifference. But how curious once more to hear a French book described as "naïve and good-natured" in comparison with the "sorrowful refinement" of a German work! [1] . . . .*

You are so right in saying that the relatively gratifying result of the election amounts to staying with existing mediocrity.[2] Wallace, certainly no great man, nevertheless has a vision of new necessities and realizes that we cannot go on living today as if we were living day before yesterday.

Music is actually the art most remote from life and needs no concrete experience at all.[3] Chopin did not want to see anything. Mozart let old Leopold tell him about the cities through which they passed. He himself sat in the house and covered music paper with notes. Zeitblom is a parody of myself. In Adrian's attitude toward life there is more of my own than one might think —or than the reader is intended to think. The book is inexpressibly close to my heart. On top of all I have been so depraved as to write the story of its genesis.

* One paragraph omitted; cf. Introduction, p. 29.

The descriptions of the countryside and the stories connected therewith call for extreme gratitude.[4] Please put up with this hasty reply! "For I am nigh o'erwhelmed with scribing"—to talk Kumpfish.[5]

Yours,

THOMAS MANN.

⊲[40]⊳

1550 San Remo Drive
Pacific Palisades, California
November 7, 1950

Dear Dr. Amann:

Thank you for your, as always, interesting letter.[1] I can now respond to your kind birthday greetings much better, or at least relatively better, than would have been possible if you had reached me then in Zürich, where I had to chop my way out of the thickest of the correspondence by means of a printed card. But those were dear, good days there, among old friends and with children and grandchildren. On June 5 I delivered in the Schauspielhaus, before a truly resplendent and gala public, the lecture you know,[2] and the following evening everyone gathered in one of the old guild houses by the Limmat for a banquet which I still remember with pleasure, thanks to speeches of high quality and imbued with real friendliness which "spiced" it (Fritz Strich,[3] Helbling,[4] de Salis [5]). Even a delegation from Lübeck [6] (!) had come to Zürich with a marzipan the size of a wagon

116

wheel. In short, nothing was lacking. In the succession of festivities what would have interested *you* most was the affair at the Sorbonne in Paris (in the big amphitheater) at which Vermeil [7] and Boucher,[8] the specialists in German literature, and Jules Romains [9] spoke. They all speak so wonderfully there. To be sure, the feeling indicated in your gifted enclosure, *"Je voudrais m'en aller,"* is never entirely lacking on such occasions. Moreover, beforehand at Flinker's bookshop I had to sign books publicly for a full three hours, especially *Le Docteur Faustus,* and was so tired at the celebration that in my speech of thanks I called Jules Romains—Romain Rolland, which of course extraordinarily heightened the general good humor—except his, I am afraid, although his smile was extremely gracious.

We spent a great deal of time with Hermann Hesse, first in Montagnola and then in Sils Maria. He is a dear old man, sly, kindly, and wise, exemplary in his stability, even in the present division of the world. Erasmean insight into the rightness and wrongness of both parties is still less proscribed and perilous in Switzerland than here, where the 38th parallel beyond which deportation threatens is rapidly crossed. But undoubtedly the fact is that "we" ought never in any circumstances have ventured to cross it.[10]

After our return home I was fearfully worn out for some time from the many changes of place, atmosphere, and altitude. Since my vigor has returned I have employed it to quickly finish the long-neglected little novel, *The Holy Sinner*—freely, very freely, after Hartmann von Aue. It is nothing special, a postlude. The time of

Magic Mountains and *Faustuses* is past. Good that at least they were. Now one only continues to entertain oneself, as best one may.

Sincerely yours,
THOMAS MANN.

⟨ 41 ⟩
[Picture postcard]

December 23, 1950

Dear Mr. Amann:

Thank you for your beautiful, earnest card, and a cordial return of your wishes! This is a part of our garden. Foolish, isn't it?

Yours,
THOMAS MANN.

⟨ 42 ⟩
[Picture postcard]

March 29, 1951

Dear Dr. Amann:

I am grateful for your letter [1] and deeply moved by your In memoriam.[2] I am ridiculously involved in work on the continuation of *Felix Krull,* and have so much to write incidentally that I—cannot write much. A copy of *Der Erwählte* [*The Holy Sinner*] is on its way to you directly from Frankfurt. You will see that on the whole I have stuck fairly closely to Oud Hartmann. And yet he would open his eyes.—This is my *piano à queue.*[3]

Cordially yours,

THOMAS MANN.

◄[43]►

1550 San Remo Drive
Pacific Palisades, California
June 3, 1951

Dear Dr. Amann:

Many thanks for the letter and picture. I am repaying you as well as I can with two photos that show my wife and myself with our eldest grandchild as a baby.[1] He is already 10½ now. In contrast to him we, at least so it seems to me, have changed little.

The Holy Sinner is an experiment, and as such succeeded quite prettily, but of course it will not bear repeating. Only people should not be so ready to take that sort of thing for a blind alley in which the author will now be caught for all eternity. I have been in many a blind alley [2] from which there was no going on, and have always managed to escape freely into something new.

The linguistic jests have nothing to do with my fate as an exile, or at any rate not the old French ones! I simply could not help imagining the supranational Middle Ages, which I was drawing in the book, as anything but a linguistic potpourri. Middle High German poetry, after all, was fond of incorporating fragments of French. That the fishermen of the Channel Islands (which do belong to Britain) should speak North Sea Low German with a dash of English is a humorous idea that will offend only those who do not understand a joke. *"Dat's nu'n little bit tau veel verlangt"* [3] is perfectly natural, you know. "Dat's" (That's) is in itself virtually English, and the "'n little bit" does not stick out in the slightest, but goes very smoothly along with the rest. But the basis is Hartmann's Middle High German—and here is the connecting link with *Faustus,* with little Echo [4] whose Swiss dialect extends the linguistic perspective of the novel beyond the baroque and the German of Luther deep into Middle High German. [5] A real critic would observe and point out such connections, instead of stupidly carping and caviling, or else spitting venom, as the anonymous of the *Supplement* seems to have done again. [6] It is always the same malignant enemy, a German, of course; as far as I know, his name is Hellmann. If only he would cease to trouble himself with such a corrupter of true art as myself! But it is a kind of hate link, originally not without other elements; an unfortunate case.—The article would interest me. Could you not send it to me? [7] If not, no great matter.

I wish you a good voyage to your son and grandson! We too shall set out for Europe again, this time in midsummer, I think, later than usual. To be candid, the shorter my time grows, the more I am drawn toward the old soil over there.[8] I have a kind of irrational horror of "resting," when the time comes, in this ground which has given me nothing and means nothing to me. I have become completely alienated from Germany. But I should really like to have my stone in Switzerland. Only that will be very difficult to arrange.

Cordially yours,

THOMAS MANN.

⊰[44]⊱

Pacific Palisades
October 9, 1951

Dear Dr. Amann:

We have just returned, and I find here your as always so kind and well-turned letter. My thanks must be insufficient, for I am, as Luther so expressively says, "overladen, overcrowded, and overpowered with affairs." [1] I quote that frequently. I must confess that I would not so readily have placed your quotation (in spite of being well acquainted with Brentano) if I had not received, simultaneously with your letter, an essay by a certain Wolfgang F. Michael of the University of Texas on E. T. A. Hoffmann and T. M.,[2] in which the sentence is also cited.[3] Professor Michael wondered whether it might not also have been written by me. I doubt it; the tone is different, and I do not like the image of the enlarged liver.[4] But I certainly have ironically slandered and mistrusted the role of the artist and writer often enough, and I suppose that the common Romantic element is that. Incidentally, I should like to put the cautious question whether Gottfried Keller might not also have written the sentence.

As for my relationship to Romanticism, the most detailed and intelligent study of it is: Käte Hamburger, "T. M. und die Romantik." (*Neue Forschung, Arbeiten zur Geistesgeschichte der germanischen und romanischen Völker,* Berlin, Junker & Dünnhaupt.) [5] I myself have made so many scattered remarks and confessions on the subject that the dictum of His Majesty, "Classicism is health and Romanticism is sickness," [6] is extremely painful to one "who loves Romanticism even to its sins and vices." [7] Certainly there were plenty of these, but I do not have so much against it as He, who after all was not always so entirely "healthy" either. My "relationship to Romanticism" can be reduced to my relationship to sickness, which I, with Nietzsche, have always regarded very highly as a source of creativity. [8]

No one would be more delighted than I if a new edition of *Tradition und Weltkrise* [9] should come about. . . .*

Yours,

Thomas Mann.

* Three sentences omitted; cf. Introduction, p. 29.

⊲[45]⊳

1550 San Remo Drive
Pacific Palisades, California
November 7, 1951

Dear Dr. Amann:

Forgive me for thanking you only now for your last friendly letter. My dislike of dictating brings me again and again in oppressive arrears with my correspondence, and often to the verge of bankruptcy. Do not punish me with too long an interval between your own letters. They are always brilliant and stimulating, and I would dearly love to sit down each time and answer them at once, but cannot manage it.

I am very sorry that you will not be able to hear Michael.[1] He has developed into a musician who deserves to be taken very seriously, and the programs of the two were attractive for their unconventionality. But I am afraid that Yalta's [2] auto accident, with the accompanying injury to her head and hand, will stop her pianistic activity for some time, and a new accompanist is not so easy to find. For the present all concerts have been canceled.

Riemer's *Mitteilungen über Goethe* [*Communications on Goethe*], edited by Pollmer (Insel, 1921) strangely enough inhabits my library in two separate copies, both of which are liberally underlined with pencil. The portrait of Riemer by Seidler [3] is certainly in the book, but as far as I recall was not in my mind when I wrote the scene.[4] I see that I knew little about him, for example, nothing about Frau von Humboldt.[5] I knew that

123

he had quarreled with August, but left it out in order to keep the cause of bitterness "pure." I really could scarcely say how I put together my portrait of him. I simply stylized him as one of the "victims," with his protestations couched in the language of praise.⁶ I still think it the best scene in the book. And at the time of writing I had a fearful attack of sciatica! ⁷

Cordially yours,
THOMAS MANN.

⊲[46]⊳

1550 San Remo Drive
Pacific Palisades, California
December 23, 1951

Dear Dr. Amann:

A thousand thanks for your richly chatty letter ¹ and for the Riemer study. I have not the slightest objection to make against anything in it, nor to the quotations from the letter,² although not much more emerges from them than that I did not really know the answer myself. The essay is decidedly interesting, and if *Modern Language* had not published several things on me quite recently, I would have no doubt of its being accepted there. In any case it is a handsome comparison between history and poesy (tolerant toward the latter) and ought to appear in print.

I have written all sorts of additions to the Krull memoirs,³ but am always running the risk of falling into a

"Faustian" sprawl and losing control of the form. Thus I bring the hero, who is an amorist, into contact with the idea of Being itself, which perhaps is only an episode between Nothingness and Nothingness, as life on earth is only an incident with beginning and end, since the inhabitability of a planet is limited. At the same time all things pass without precise boundaries into one another: Man into the animal realm, the latter into the vegetable realm, organic into inorganic being, the material into the immaterial, into scarcely-yet-being and into non-being, without space and time. Primal creation: How and when did the first vibration of being (electromagnetic or whatever) appear in the void? This is the true primal creation, the first newness. The second is that addition to the inorganic which we call life, something added without any addition of matter. A third addition in the realm of the organic and animal is the human element. Transition is observed, but something indefinable comes in, as when the turning point to "life" was reached. Love, understood as sensual stirring by the transitory quality of Being, not only of life, not only of man. And Being itself, then, perhaps an evocation by love out of the void?—Nonsense, you don't understand a word.[4] A small grandson of mine said as he came out of church: "When you start to think about God, you get combustion of the brain." A new phrase, and not a bad one.

I beg your pardon and wish you very happy holidays.

Yours,

THOMAS MANN.

⋅[47]⋅

1550 San Remo Drive
Pacific Palisades, California
June 19, 1952

Dear Dr. Amann:

Be forbearing with me! Your letters are always such stimulating, knowledgeable and thoughtful impromptus, and I keep up with you so poorly. For weeks I have not been really well and lack energy. Intestinal spasms, gastric weakness, and lack of appetite have run me down. I am hoping for betterment in the Swiss mountains in July, and at Gastein, where we intend to take a cure in August. We are leaving here on the 24th, and there are a thousand things to do beforehand.

My European address is: Zürich, Hotel Baur au lac, or else c/o Europa Verlag, Rämistrasse 5.

I also intend to go to Rome in September, in order to thank the Accademia dei Lincei [1] for the International Literature Prize, which they have conferred on me. And yet only recently, when I was rereading Tolstoy's *Haji Murad,* I felt like a mouse in comparison to such a lion.

Rest assured that every letter which comes from you is a joy and precious entertainment to me! [2]

Yours,
Thomas Mann.

⊲[48]⊳

Waldhaus Dolder
Zürich
December 1, 1952

Thank you for your as always delightful letter of October.[1] I have been away from P. P.[2] since June, traveled a great deal since, and am now settled down here. For next year we have rented a small house in Erlenbach above the lake and want to resume the pattern our life took between 1933 and 1938. "Passing of the declining years and literary activity"—that is how the residence permit puts it, and puts it nicely, after all.

Yours,
Thomas Mann.

Appendix, Notes, and Index of Persons

Appendix

Draft of a letter from Paul Amann to Thomas Mann, undated: February or March, 1915:

Draft; clean copy was mailed at once.
Dear Herr Thomas Mann:

Your reply was a pure, intense joy to me. To find you as I had imagined the author of *The Infant Prodigy;* the possibility of extending to you, from my modest, diligently turned-up field, a small gift in return for such precious, sharp pleasures, and to have it accepted so affably—all that has done me a great deal of good.

I had tolerably well guessed the motives for your polemic: [1] what so many professors (alas, I too am one of the crew), what even Gerhart Hauptmann [2] attempted unskillfully or feebly, had to be done once more with trenchant acuity. A matter of a duel. I slept away in Galicia this dreadful period; it may be that if I were capable of what you are capable, I would have done something similar; for me it would have been the problem of Corneille's Cid.

Even if there were some way of doing so, I should

not have said publicly what I believed I had to say to you. But the time may come when it will be one's duty, come what may come, to make a strong stand against political, historical, psychological prejudices whose effects might postpone the future peace, or again fatally poison it.

Toward a strong opponent I could allow myself to be one-sided, especially if the fragment of truth at stake could not be brought to light otherwise. What you say about "justice" is so fine! Objectivity is superstition—except in bacteriology, chemistry, etc. (and not even there: personal jealousies come up). Yet the obligation remains to avoid conscious falsifications of one's own judgment. But otherwise, in questions in which the ego with its demands can enter in any way (and where does it not do so?), one must treat oneself as the scientist does his instruments, taking into account ultimate sources of error and correcting opinions accordingly. Not in order to put one's conscience at rest, but so that the greatest possible part of what has been discovered will stand the test of time, will be close to the truth.

The scholar's insights, like the artist's creative work, ought to stand above the desire for personal fulfillment. Even where he *is* being objective, he will experience uneasiness at feeling himself to be partial; he may only be acknowledging the dicta of the intellect, but his intellectual origins, the choice of his field of study, the rhythm of his work, his urge to pass judgment, his vision, and his discoveries, flow out of his life—which is really not legitimate. But even in the greatest Germans this connection of understanding with subjectivism is only too obvious. You spoke, for example, of German self-criticism. Goethe,

Schopenhauer, Nietzsche, sometimes Bismarck, too—men
who produced the most forceful examples of German self-
criticism—spoke as men who had been misunderstood,
hampered; vexation and bitterness sharpened their insight. But for that very reason a large part of what they
said may well be *true*.

You use Bismarck's strong phrase; [3] to deny that the
underlying motive of your essay was the quest for justice.
But you also do me too much honor when you assume that
I, for my part, should have wanted above all to be just.
Such lofty abstractions do not go well in German, not for
me either. My impulse came from the métier, the compul-
sion of the craftsman to take a hand when he finds work
half or wrongly done, a feeling for logical balance, at
bottom even a dogma whose existence I frankly confess:
it is a kind of analogy to Robert Meyer's [4] hypothesis of
the conservation of energy, extended to the fields of culture and psychology. A fairly good eye for intellectual
forces keeps me from explaining the world-wide anger
at our fatherland as simply the result of base motives plus
ignorance. Old Fontane's favorite phrase, "Those who
live on the other side of the mountain are people, too,"
also belongs among the dogmas of which I am not
ashamed. To that must be added a third motto whose
formulation I owe to Rolland: *L'idéalisme de chaque
nation est fait d'un peu de vérité et de beaucoup de men-
songe.* And I add: Until proved otherwise it must be as-
sumed that the worth-while people of all degrees exist
in equal proportions in all the nations with which we are
associated. That does not mean that at every given moment these nations are of equal value (for they may man-

age well or ill with the things at their command, the result being periods of flowering or decadence). Nor does it mean that these value-determining individuals are altogether alike without regard to frontiers.

If these premises were proved false, I should abandon my studies and cultivate cabbage—not out of rancor, but because there would then be nothing to be done. If that were so, one would have only the alternatives of draping one's own egoism in the guise of scholarship or, with a single leap, even that of a foreign nation (Gobineau, Houston Stewart Chamberlain, A. Bonus, *et tutti quanti*).

Right now I want to go back to one special point that you stress: my comment on Rolland's present development. As you quote my words, they sound alien to me and have a hollow ring à la Victor Hugo—you are right about that. But that is only *my* fault; I should have expressed myself more clearly. I cannot assume that you are familiar with Rolland's *Jean-Christophe*. If you do know the work, however, and still put Rolland alongside Hugo, then I should only have to regard your doing so as one more example of the empirical rule that great artists, despite their ability to understand art entirely from within, are not the fairest critics. Indeed, often they cannot be, and I should have to value your opinion simply as a specific reaction of your own specific qualities as an artist. But I do not think you really know Rolland's work. Similarly there is no point in my explaining why, to my mind, Hugo represents France's nether pole, and Rolland a peak achievement of the French spirit, death and life. You think it is shameful that in the midst of this grave struggle he devotes himself to the effort of achieving spiritual forms of community life without the necessity of a state (this is a later development than his Cossack essay; [5] I know little about it and can likewise not entirely follow him in such an endeavor). You find the gesture typically French—so do I, only we evaluate it differently. Thanks to my "dogmas" I force myself to take the great European nations equally seriously; I do not think that life has a lesser specific gravity anywhere. Everything that may be said against the French can stand, nothing need be withdrawn; but I see distinctly the polarity in the existence of every nation. Life is comedy and tragedy everywhere; and every nation has its tragic conflict—and its tragic dignity. So that we may come to a quick understanding on this matter—may I ask you to look at the last half-page of your essay,[6] at the top, the first sentence? (I do not have the magazine here.) And in that sentence consider the *origin* of all the *emphatic words*. The result: the thought and the language is French. This fine, lofty sentence displays affinities with English; the entire upper neurological tract is French.[7] (Please believe that this is not intended as puristic criticism.) Other example: I am reading in the Bismarck book published by Langewiesche Verlag a scene in which Bismarck censures careless work with the remark: "What a cavalier has undertaken to do is already as good as done."[8] The phrasing and the manner of thought are classically French. As a result of Colbert's action, of the *refugiés,* of Frederick the Great, and of Stein's adaptation of the ideas of the Revolution, Prussia was fourfold created out of the French spirit, out of French blood. Ricarda Huch's "great war" shows what the German princes were without French discipline. The only refined one, the Landgrave of Hessen, was a Calvinist, and only the addition of the ferment of Calvinism enabled Prussia to convert her Lutheranism into an institution useful to the State. That is not wild Gallomania, though it may seem so, nor is it in any way to the dishonor of a country that has produced a Goethe, a Bismarck, a Beethoven. No Frenchman would judge it so. Is it an abuse of your kindness if I ask permission to "derive" the matter concisely in good German fashion "from its first principles"?

Modern Europe is founded upon the power, the development of the individual. Viewed from this point of view, classical France is reactionary, even alien to Europe. (W. Lowell, *The Soul of the Far East,*[9] places her alongside Japan.) For she aimed for the subordination, the elimination of individualism. (La Bruyère [10] commends Racine for the fact that in society one could not observe any sign of his being an *homme de lettres*. Or in the *Princesse de Clèves* [11] a clever mother dismisses a certain delicacy of feeling in her daughter as *opinion particulière.*) However, this subordination is demanded (and that again is brightly occidental) not dogmatically, but in the name of the spiritual force of *raison* common to all. Thus this culture is capable of creating social values of *every* shading, or at least was capable of doing so in its two periods of historical culmination: at the time of chivalric and Gothic culture, and then again in the seventeenth and early eighteenth century. During those epochs it created—and this can be easily shown—the form and content of the noblest types of European life. But it was not merely a culture of the salon or the tournament; Bernard of Clairvaux, the Carthusians, the Trappists, Port-Royal, illustrate the profoundest earnestness. If you read *Jung Stillings Leben* or *Anton Reiser* by Goethe's friend Ph. Moritz, you will find, as the sources from which Westphalian peasants or Brunswickian artisans draw their deeply felt pietism—none other than Fénelon [12] and Guyon! [13] And so on to infinity, in all departments of living values. Why should that be so? In higher matters the individualistic Germans cannot be reduced to a common denominator—unless it is a foreign one. Among us, reason stands in such ill repute in the *highest* realms of creativity that socially valid creativity is not possible; at most, brutal instinctual fads travel through the country and across the border: anti-Semitism, Germanomania. From sense of self-preservation the German is more and more learning how to exclude his emotions from common work. Hence the machinelike precision. Bismarck again says that in politics one must be as dead to feeling as Richard III.

The principle rouses both horror and admiration. It is said that at the Masurian Lakes nine regimental bands drowned out the whimpering of the Russians perishing in the marsh, so that the Germans would not become nervous. Socially, culturally, therefore, Germany cannot easily begin—or end—anything. Without Napoleon the old German Empire was still dragging on an invalid existence. Very frequently the impulse toward something new came from the West; very seldom did a rejuvenating wave of humanity or feeling pour back to the West in compensation. That sums up the mutual relationship of the two countries.

Think of recent examples: Aviation and submarine technology began in France and thence traveled to the rest of the world. We learned these techniques with considerable difficulty—but ultimately better, more thoroughly, more boldly.

Try now as a psychologist to deduce the psychic stratifications of such a reciprocal relationship. The French: a people of fashion, of changing tastes, of cyclonic social currents, little subject to the spell of powerful personalities, nervous, skeptical, fanatical, artistic, for whole half-millennia needing nothing from the neighbor, therefore knowing him only as a client, a customer. And then one day this nation is suddenly overwhelmed physically or spiritually by the neighbor (Staël, *Allemagne*) without really understanding why. And then the Germans: materially powerful, incessantly keeping an eye on the others for fear that without them she will be socially, even spiritually brutalized, rusticated. (Today there is too much of the French heritage in cold storage in Germany for that to happen again, as it did in the fourteenth century.) At the same time the Germans can tell themselves in justified pride that they are, as human beings, more powerful, more efficient, more firmly fixed in themselves. They will naturally come to think, again and again, that only this constant peering across the border stands in the way of their ultimate cultural unfolding; while in fact it is precisely their greater share of individualism, their joy in luxuriant offshoots, which is to blame for their incapacity to achieve independent, self-initiated progress as a whole. Out of an incredible variety of initial steps toward progress there emerges, without some foreign contribution, only anarchy; a usable program has to be delivered from outside Germany. I have discovered that myself in connection with this very subject. I would never have found this formulation—even though I recognized all sorts of evidence for it in a vague and premonitory way—without the aid of a certain piece of French writing. It is a book which takes issue with certain venerable and worn-out clichés, and although one might dispute it on certain points, as a whole it is a *rocher de bronze.* I am referring to Raynaud's [14] *Histoire générale de l'Influence française en l'Allemagne,* 1914. For quick orientation the preambles to the chapters suffice; most of the actual details are correct, as far as I have been able to check them.

I have been too loquacious again; for that reason I shall deal with the territorial question simply by setting down two quotations. General von Kretschman [15] (the father of Lily Braun) writes in his war letters of 1870–1871, p. 216: "I am not in favor of large annexations of territory; why close our eyes to the experience we have had so frequently, that it is not good to force people who are French to become Germans. I would be content with Alsatia, that is, with a narrow strip of land along the French eastern border . . ." P. 344: "The bite is in my opinion more than we can digest." That noble fellow Max Eyth (*Im Strome der Welt*) [16] uses almost the same words, and in the same breath offers himself as a candidate for espionage in Le Havre. Gustav Freytag, too, is not in favor of the annexation of Lorraine; even Bismarck speaks of "professor's ideas" when Erwin von Steinbach's [17] opinions are thrown at him. He wanted some territory in hostage because he considered the French irreconcilable—and perhaps wanted to have them so. At any rate, these considerations are *not* refuted by the fact that the French remained irreconcilable; those who had the decisions to make in those days were not aiming for reconciliation. "Listening to reason," that is to say, renouncing the idea of power, is death for a big power; such renunciation can be honorably achieved only by an escape from modern statehood (a fashion that is not even three centuries old). That is what Rolland seems to be trying for.

I hope that you do not regret your kind response to my letter; I do think a private exchange of ideas like this is a necessity nowadays. I do *not in the least* represent Austria; I stand quite alone. Everything in this country is more popish than the pope. Our noble Kürnberger [18] spoke in 1870 of the "brutish incapacity" of the French to understand any kind of metaphysics. We are hearing that sort of thing again.

> With cordial gratitude,
> Yours,
> DR. AMANN.

[On the margin:]
I am looking forward eagerly to your Frederick essay in the *Rundschau.*

Notes

[The translators wish to thank Dr. Paul Scherrer, head of the Thomas Mann Archives at the Federal Institute of Technology in Zürich, Switzerland, and his assistants Fräulein Edith Egli and Fräulein Ursina Pestalozzi, for their generous help in keying these notes to editions of Thomas Mann's works in English.]

Frequently cited library sources and their abbreviations.

Amann, Paul: *Politik und Moral in Thomas Manns "Betrachtungen eines Unpolitischen."* In: *Münchner Blätter für Dichtung und Graphik,* Jahrgang 1, 1919, pp. 25–32, 42–48. Abbreviated: *Politik und Moral.*

Amann, Paul: *Tradition und Weltkrise.* Berlin, 1934. Abbreviated: *Tradition.*

Kantorowicz, Alfred: *Heinrich und Thomas Mann,* Berlin, 1956. Abbreviated: Kantorowicz.

Mann, Thomas: *Betrachtungen eines Unpolitischen.* Berlin, 1918. Abbreviated: *Betrachtungen.*

Mann, Thomas: *Frederick and the Great Coalition.* In *Three Essays,* New York: Alfred A. Knopf, Inc., 1929. Abbreviated: *Frederick.*

Mann, Thomas: *Gedanken im Kriege* (abbreviated: *Gedanken*) and *An die Redaktion des "Svenska Dag-*

141

bladet," Stockholm, (abbreviated: *Svenska*). Contained in the volume, *Friedrich und die grosse Koalition,* Berlin, 1915, to which page numbers refer.

Mann, Thomas: *Introduction to "The Magic Mountain" for Students of Princeton University.* Printed under the title of "The Making of *The Magic Mountain*" in the one-volume edition of that work published by Alfred A. Knopf, Inc., New York, 1958. (Abbreviated: *Princeton.*)

Mann, Thomas: *A Sketch of my Life,* Harrison of Paris, 1930. (Abbreviated: *Sketch.*)

Mann, Victor: *Wir Waren Fünf. Bildnis der Familie Mann.* Konstanz, 1949. (Abbreviated: Viktor Mann.)

Rolland, Romain: *Au-dessus de la mêlée.* Paris, 1915. (Abbreviated: *Au-dessus.*)

NOTES TO THE INTRODUCTION

1. Amann, *Tradition,* p. 34.
2. *Ibid.*
3. *Op. cit.,* p. 16.
4. On *Tradition* cf. the discussion by Hermann Hesse referred to in Note 8 to Letter 34, and one by Ludwig Feuchtwanger in the *Jüdische Rundschau* for November 30, 1934.
5. Amann was the recipient of some eighty letters from Romain Rolland between 1911 and 1938. These, like the letters of Thomas Mann, were in the keeping of his friend the Viennese librarian Dr. Otto Brechler, and survived the Second World War (according to letters from Amann dated May 1, 1956, and May 22, 1957).
6. Thus in the undated copy of a letter from Amann to Thomas Mann written in the summer of 1948.
7. Thus in "The Years of My Life," *Harper's Magazine,*

October, 1950, p. 256; and *Sketch*, p. 49. Cf. also
Letter 31.

8. *Politik und Moral*, p. 44, col. 1.
9. Characteristic of this is the fact that Amann wrote a long
   letter from Sarajevo during Easter of 1916, in which
   he defended Germany, her policies, and her methods
   of warfare (especially in regard to Belgium) against
   the charges of the Allies.
10. *Loc. cit.*, p. 29, col. 2, and especially p. 44 ff.
11. *Politik und Moral*, p. 46, col. 2.
12. Letter 19; cf. Amann's *Politik und Moral*, p. 29, col. 2.
13. *Politik und Moral*, p. 44, col. 2.
14. Letter 16.
15. Letter 31.
16. *Politik und Moral*, p. 45, col. 1.
17. *Sketch*, p. 47.
18. In the *Mitteilungen der literarhistorischen Gesellschaft
    in Bonn*, Jahrgang 11, Heft 4, p. 84.
19. *Sketch*, p. 47.
20. Letter 15.
21. Letter 9.
22. Letter 22 and Note 12.
23. *Die Entstehung des Doktor Faustus*, 1949, p. 201.
24. Letter 31.
25. Letters 33 and 34.
26. Letter 46.
27. Letters 39 and 40.

NOTES TO THE LETTERS

[1]

1. A newly built house in Munich-Bogenhausen into which
   the Thomas Mann family moved in 1914. "On the
   edge of the ducal park, which had just been opened
   up for building purposes, quite close to the Isar, which

at this point spills foaming over shallow cascades."
(Viktor Mann, p. 346; cf. also Thomas Mann,
Sketch, p. 46.)

2. The correspondence was initiated by Amann in January,
1915 (cf. Introduction, p. 13). Amann's first letter,
which has not been preserved, was still remembered
and praised by Thomas Mann in October, 1916 (Letter 17: "For seldom did anything strike me as more
intelligent than your letter . . .") Concerning
Amann's later statement (*Politik und Moral,* p. 46,
col. 2) that Thomas Mann quoted from this letter in
the *Betrachtungen,* p. 136, cf. Introduction, p. 18.

3. *Gedanken,* first printed in the *Neue Rundschau,* 1914,
November issue, pp. 1471–1484, then included in
the book containing the essay *Friedrich,* Berlin, 1915,
pp. 7–31. References in the following notes are to
the book edition.

4. Goethe, *Maximen und Reflexionen über Literatur und
Ethik:* "The man of action is always unscrupulous;
only the onlooker has scruples." (*Werke,* I, Bd. 42,
p. 138, Sophien edition.) Thomas Mann refers to
this dictum of Goethe's, and its inversion in the case
of the artist, in the *Betrachtungen* also, p. 212; here
the rest of this thought (down to "therefore unscrupulous") is repeated almost word for word, but without
reference to the *Rundschau* article.

5. Goethe, *Dichtung und Wahrheit,* Teil 3, Buch 12
(Werke I, Bd. 28, p. 109, Sophien ed.), in connection with the discussion of Amann's principle that
everything man undertakes must spring from the to-
tality of his united energies. This, Goethe says, encounters great difficulties because ideas must be trans-
mitted by means of words.

6. The contrast between Western "civilization" and German
"culture" forms the principal subject of the *Rundschau* article.

Notes

7. Thomas Mann's mother, née Julia da Silva-Bruhns, was the "daughter of a German planter and a Portuguese-Creole Brazilian." (*Sketch*, p. 7; cf. for more detail Viktor Mann, p. 17 ff. and geneological table after p. 598. Similarly, in *Betrachtungen*, p. 134.)

8. In the speech *Germany and the Germans* (Library of Congress, 1945), p. 19, Thomas Mann still speaks of "the tendency toward self-criticism, often to the point of self-disgust and self-execration," as thoroughly German.

9. In thought and phraseology this sentence corresponds to a passage in *Svenska*, which first appeared in Germany in the June, 1915, number of the *Neue Rundschau*. Cf. p. 120 of the book edition. According to this edition, p. 131, the article was written in April, 1915. Cf. Introduction, p. 16.

10. This expression is a play on words based upon the German: *"Es ist mir Wurst"*—literally, "It's so much sausage to me"—which means approximately, "I don't give a damn." *Farcimentum* is a joking extension of the Latin *farcimen*, "sausage," and was apparently first used by Bismarck in Versailles on January 21, 1871. Concluding a discussion of the controversy over possible titles for the German Kaiser, Bismarck said: *"Farcimentum or farcimen, it's all one. Nescio quid mihi magis farcimentum esset."* (Moritz Busch, *Graf Bismarck und seine Leute während des Kriegs mit Frankreich*, Bd. 2, 1878, p. 255.)

11. Cf. the remark of Naphta in his long tirade against justice (*The Magic Mountain*, New York: Alfred A. Knopf, Inc., 1958, p. 691.)

12. In his reply (reprinted here in the Appendix) Amann contests this assumption, declaring that he does not in the least represent Austria, and that in Austria everything is "more popish than the pope" (i.e., more German in spirit than the Germans of the Reich).

13. At this time the dispute mentioned in the Introduction
(p. 20) between Thomas Mann and Rolland had already come into the open. Rolland had been attacked
by Mann in *Gedanken* for the "outrageously impermissible ignorance concerning Germany which speaks
. . . out of every utterance by Bergson, Maeterlinck,
Rolland, Richepin, Deschanel, Pichon and Churchill."
Rolland's counterblast against Thomas Mann was
printed in the *Journal de Genève* for December 4,
1914 (and later reprinted in the collection of essays,
Au-dessus, Paris, 1915, p. 131 f.). Thomas Mann
could have seen it by the time he wrote the present
letter.

14. Amann firmly rejects the comparison between Rolland
and Hugo in his reply. See Appendix.

15. Thomas Mann's attention may have been called to this
by an article in the feuilleton section of his favorite
Frankfurter Zeitung for February 6, 1915: *Eine
Schmähschrift der Akademie der Wissenschaften von
Portugal gegen Deutschland*. This article also re-
printed an extract, in translation, from Anatole
France's message to the president of the Academy,
Theophil Braga.

16. In his article *Au-dessus,* first printed in the *Journal de
Genève* for September 15, 1914, Rolland had hailed
the heroic, self-sacrificing youth of all nations, including the "Germans who are fighting to defend the intellect and the city of Kant against the torrent of
Cossack horsemen."

17. Similarly in *Gedanken,* p. 30, in which Thomas Mann
speaks of "all the impudent plotting" of the Allies
against Germany.

18. *Frederick,* according to Thomas Mann's own statement
in the German edition, was written in December,
1914.

Notes

[2]

1. For the draft of this letter, see Appendix.
2. The draft of Amann's letter does not contain an appreciation of the *Frederick* essay, which he had not seen at the time of writing. He must have added comments to the clean copy, unless he quickly sent a separate letter. Even in *Politik und Moral*, p. 25, Amann had words of warm acknowledgment and understanding for *Frederick*.
3. *Frederick;* cf. Note 18 to Letter 1.
4. Samuel Fischer, Berlin, whose publishing house that year brought out the essay, together with *Gedanken* and *Svenska* in a collection of contemporary documents entitled *Sammlung von Schriften zur Zeitgeschichte.*
5. The idea that Prussianism must be discarded after the war also appears, although in somewhat more tentative form, in *Svenska*. Here Thomas Mann writes; "Infinitely wiser concerning herself and others . . . Germany, when she has withstood this trial, will no longer need to build as she has done previously upon Prussianism, the principle of power, but will be able to afford the cheerful luxury, the joy . . . of the liberal spirit."
6. Echoes of these phrases in *Svenska,* p. 139; somewhat remoter echoes in *Betrachtungen,* p. 28.
7. Sir Edward Grey, after 1916 Viscount Grey of Fallodon, British Foreign Secretary from 1905 to 1916. The reference is probably to his speech of March 23, 1915, in which he said: "Since the beginning of the war we have learned the German ideal from German professors and publicists. It is this, that the Germans are a superior people to whom all that leads to power is permitted and against whom any resistance is wrong."
8. The following sentences recur, word for word in some

instances, in *Svenska*, p. 123 f. The following notes call attention to occasional softening of the phraseology in the article.

9. In the article, more cautiously: "that Might may in fact be considered Right" (p. 123).

10. Here, too, less sharply: "For some time she has been regarded as brutal, but in order to achieve some degree of psychological fairness about her, it must be realized that the brutality in question has sprung from intellectuality" (p. 123).

11. This sentence and the two sentences in parentheses are not included in the article.

12. The article mentions only Kant's "practical reason" and does not mention "Luther's concessions."

13. "Rather brutal" is not in the article.

14. The expressions "democratization of Germany" and (in the last clause) "democratic world culture" are not used in the article.

[3]
1. The passage reads: "Their lordships the artists are far from having so independent a posture in the world and against the world that their opinions and changes of opinion in themselves merit attention. They have been at all times the lackeys of some morality or philosophy or religion." (Nietzsche, *Zur Genealogie der Moral*, Gesammelte Werke, Bd. 15, pp. 376–377, Musarion edition.)

[4]
1. Klaus Mann, 1906–1949. This is probably the illness described several years later in *Gesang vom Kindchen*, Munich, 1919–1920, p. 8.

2. Details about the Tölz country house in Viktor Mann, p. 349, and in *Sketch*, p. 35.

3. Marie Jean Antoine Nicolas Caritat, Marquis de Condorcet, 1743–1794, mathematician and philosopher, member of the Academy of Sciences, president of the National Assembly in 1792. As a Girondist he was indicted, arrested, and died in prison, probably from poison. Amann, who helped us to decipher the rather illegible name in the text of the letter, wrote in comment that he had hoped to interest Thomas Mann in the story of Condorcet, whose moving last days might have made an excellent essay, lending itself to somewhat the same treatment that Mann had given Schiller. Condorcet was hiding before his arrest when he wrote his principal work, an optimistic view of the future of humanity: *Esquisse d'un tableau historique des progrès de l'esprit humain.*

4. Similarly it is said of Gustav von Aschenbach that his works were "heaped up to greatness in layer after layer, in long days of work, out of hundreds and hundreds of single inspirations." (*Death in Venice,* New York: Alfred A. Knopf, Inc., 1930, p. 18.) Similarly of Richard Wagner: "Two hours daily. By such small stages, then, at least at times, this whole gigantic life-work is erected [heaped up]; struggling all the time against rapidly supervening exhaustion . . ." ("Sufferings and Greatness of Richard Wagner," in *Essays of Three Decades,* New York: Alfred A. Knopf, Inc., 1948, p. 325.)

5. The work on *The Magic Mountain* began in 1912 (*Sketch,* p. 43).

6. This confirms the correctness of later statements on the planning of *The Magic Mountain.* Likewise in *Princeton,* p. 722, Thomas Mann speaks of the plan for a "companion-piece to *Death in Venice* and was to be about the same length," and in *Sketch,* p. 43, of a "short tale." On the other hand in a letter to Amann of March, 1917 (Letter 22), he is already speaking

of a novel, and likewise in the *Betrachtungen,* p. 426, "a small novel" is mentioned.

7. This passage is probably the earliest use of the phrase "sympathy with death" (cf. *The Magic Mountain,* 1958 ed., p. 652). The phrase is employed in the *Betrachtungen,* p. 426, to define a thematic component of the novel in being, and on page 427 sympathy with death is called the "formula and underlying tendency of all Romanticism."

8. The title is not mentioned in the *Betrachtungen,* but as Thomas Mann writes in *Princeton,* p. 722, "from the very first the tale bore that title."

9. On the significance of the outbreak of the war of 1914 not only for the conclusion of *The Magic Mountain* but also for its total conception, cf. Thomas Mann's remarks in his *Neue Studien,* 1948, p. 163.

10. Similarly, in the *Betrachtungen,* p. 191 f.: "I also see quite well how the story *Death in Venice* is fixed in its period, fixed shortly before the war in its tension of the will and its morbidity; in its way there is a finality to it . . ."

11. There is some discrepancy between this and the account of the order of his creative work on the eve of the war given by Thomas Mann in *Sketch,* p. 40, and *Princeton,* p. 722; he states therein that *Death in Venice* and then *The Magic Mountain* interrupted the work on the Krull memoirs.

12. According to the *Sketch,* p. 39, the work on *Felix Krull* began immediately after completion of *Royal Highness,* that is, around 1910. This is confirmed by the letter to Heinrich Mann of January 10, 1910 (in Kantorowicz, p. 85): "I am collecting, taking notes and making studies for the confessions of a confidence man, which will probably be my strangest production." A first sample—the episode with the actor Müller-Rosé—appeared as early as 1911 in the Al-

manac of S. Fischer Verlag, *Das 25. Jahr,* pp. 273–283.

13. Similarly in *Princeton,* manuscript, p. 6: "A sort of parody of the great memoirs of the 18th century and even of Goethe's *Dichtung und Wahrheit.*" Passage cut by Thomas Mann in manuscript. Cf. also *Betrachtungen,* p. 67.

14. Cf. Note 9 to Letter 1.

15. In the feuilleton section. This article, which appeared under the heading "Gedanken zum Kriege" ["Thoughts on the War"] must be distinguished from *Gedanken im Kriege,* which was first published in the November, 1914, issue of the *Neue Rundschau.* In the article Thomas Mann expresses his conviction that the future would be determined by the German conception of the state and by German culture, not by Western civilization; he speaks also of the great pain that Western propaganda has imposed upon Germany and insists that right is on the side of Germany.

16. Similarly in a remark of Naphta's directed against Western ideas. (*The Magic Mountain,* 1958 ed., p. 691.)

17. Cf. *Gedanken,* p. 10: "That victorious bellicose principle of today: organization . . ." In the article mentioned above, Note 15, it is also mentioned as a victorious German principle recognized by Germany's foes as worth imitating. This point, too, can be regarded as part of the controversy with Romain Rolland, who in his article of December 4, 1914, in the *Journal de Genève,* "Les Idoles" (*Au-dessus,* p. 137 f.) lashed out against the German worship of organization.

[5]

1. Thomas Mann's preceding letter (No. 4) addressed to Amann's army postal number, had been stamped *sick* and redirected to his private address in Vienna.

2. *Death in Venice,* first published in the *Neue Rundschau* in 1912.
3. The reference is probably to *The Magic Mountain.*
4. Thus, for example, Richard Zimmermann in *Preussische Jahrbücher,* Bd. 156, 1914, p. 356 f.: "The novella will no doubt generally be regarded as description and confessions of the author himself . . . he indulges in a rather solemn treatment of himself." Cf. also the pamphlet by Bernd Isemann, *Thomas Mann und der Tod in Venedig,* Munich, 1913, p. 9, wherein commenting on the description of Aschenbach's daily stint Isemann writes: One feels about to suffocate in this hieratic stuffiness." Further Josef Hofmiller: *Thomas Manns neue Erzählung,* in *Süddeutsche Monatschefte,* Jahrgang 10, 1913, p. 230: "I must admit that it is embarrasing to me and seems to verge on the unendurable when Mann confers upon Aschenbach so much, so altogether too much, of himself."
5. Similarly *Betrachtungen,* p. 72: "Whereas it was a matter of adaptation, indeed of parody."
6. Ulrike von Levetzow, 1804–1899.
7. The Nietzsche passage reads: "If we wish to gather experience with art, let us make a few works of art; there is no other way to develop aesthetic judgment. Most artists are themselves useful solely because they acquire, preserve and transmit the sensibility of the great masters—much, that is, as if they were heat-conducting media." (*Kunst und Schriftstellerei,* Gesammelte Werke, Bd. 9, p. 421, Musarion edition.)
8. More detail about this in the autobiographical essay "Kinderspiele" ("Childrens' Games") in *Rede und Antwort,* 1922, p. 390.
9. This anticipates the first motto which Thomas Mann later placed at the head of *Betrachtungen: "Que diable allait-il faire dans cette galère?"* (Molière, *Les*

fourberies de Scapin, II, 11.) Cf. the similar question in *Betrachtungen,* p. 126.

10. Similarly in *Betrachtungen,* p. 150.

11. This passage appears almost word for word (up to "are with Germany today") in *Betrachtungen,* p. 346 f., in a passage written in May, 1917.

12. Similarly in Letter 1.

13. *Amusing* in the sense of the eighteenth-century rococo, with which the West is identified in Letter 4. Similarly, in Letter 2 Thomas Mann speaks of radicalism's "gallantry of gesture." Cf. also *Betrachtungen,* pp. 290 and 293, where democracy is referred to as the "amusing state"; and especially pp. 28–29: "An amusing, indeed, a thoroughly amusing Europe; not to desire that at least testifies to lack of egoism in a writer."

14. Cf. Letter 1 and *Betrachtungen,* p. 32.

15. Similarly, *Betrachtungen,* p. 11 f.: "That spirit which in the Jacobin froze into . . . murderous doctrine, tyrannical schoolmaster's pedantry."

16. Cf., in part repeated word for word, *Betrachtungen,* p. 12.

[6]

1. Concerning this, Amann wrote to us on February 12, 1956, that the "successful portrait" was probably lost in Paris in 1940 along with his refugee baggage. Under the portrait Thomas Mann had written a dozen lines taken from Amann's essay on him in the French periodical *L'Effort* (cf. Note 3 below).

2. Amann noted in pencil on the margin of this letter: "Lieutnant Schimek in Memoriam. Frkftr. Ztg. Oct. 15." In fact this essay of Amann's appeared in the *Frankfurter Zeitung* for Sunday, November 21, 1915 (Jahrg. 60, No. 323, first morning edition). The

article relates an encounter with a young Czech reserve lieutenant who soon afterward fell in battle. The lieutenant, a botanist, was, like the author, a *gymnasium* teacher by profession. The conversations of the two on the central Dniester, in the primeval forests of eastern Galicia, began with botanical observations and soon passed to more general subjects like the interrelationships of nationalities.

3. Amann noted in pencil on the margin: *"L'Effort,* weekly magazine, Poitiers, à la Mérigote, editor Jean R. Bloch, March (?), 1912. Letter on Th. Mann, Emil Strauss, Hermann Hesse." The article, which in fact treated only the first two writers, appeared under the heading *"Deux Romanciers Allemands"* in *Effort Libre,* Année 1, Cahiers 15–18, pp. 513–540. According to Amann, the suggestion for the article had come from friends of Romain Rolland. In *Betrachtungen,* p. 152, Thomas Mann mentions the article —without naming the author—in connection with a direct attack upon Romain Rolland. Two sentences are quoted here; cf. Introduction p. 18.

4. On the differences between French and German criticism of *Royal Highness,* cf. similar remarks in *Betrachtungen,* p. 61 f. The widespread lack of understanding on the part of the German critics, of which Thomas Mann was acutely conscious at the time (thus in a letter to Heinrich Mann dated January 26, 1910, in Kantorowicz, p. 86, and in the essay "Über Königliche Hoheit" reprinted in *Rede und Antwort* pp. 342–350), continued to preoccupy him in his old age (Foreword to the radio play *Royal Highness,* 1954, in *Nachlese,* pp. 170 f.)

5. In his essay "Königliche Hoheit" in *Neue Rundschau,* Jahrgang 1909, pp. 1803–1808.

6. Similarly, Thomas Mann speaks of the "milder, slacker, more 'human' atmosphere" which one felt as soon as

one crossed the border out of Germany (*Betrach-tungen,* p. 477).

7. Above in Letter 5.
8. Cf. *Royal Highness,* New York: Alfred A. Knopf, Inc., 1939, p. 175.
9. The following remarks recur, in part word for word, in the idyll *A Man and his Dog,* written in 1918. Cf. p. 443 and p. 446 in *Stories of Three Decades,* New York: Alfred A. Knopf, Inc., 1936.
10. Cf. "A Man and his Dog" in *Stories of Three Decades.*
11. Cf. also Monika Mann, *Vergangenes und Gegenwärtiges. Erinnerungen.* 1956, p. 43 f.
12. In *Royal Highness.*
13. Allusion to the Italian writer Gabriele d'Annunzio, 1863–1938, who in 1915 advocated Italy's entry into the war. Similarly, in Letter 22 Thomas Mann speaks of the Italian troops as "Gabriele's hosts." On d'Annunzio as "Latin poet-politician and warmonger" cf. also *Betrachtungen,* p. 597 f.
14. In a similar connection Thomas Mann speaks of d'Annunzio's "lascivious aestheticism" (*Betrachtungen,* p. 25).
15. The same remark in *Betrachtungen,* p. 24.
16. Similarly, Thomas Mann, who did his military service in 1900 as a "one-year volunteer," used the phrase "most amusing corruption" in describing his rapid discharge to his brother Heinrich (letter of April 27, 1912, in Kantorowicz, p. 99).
17. Similarly in *Sketch,* p. 27.
18. Field Marshal General von Mackensen, commander-in-chief of the German Eleventh and the Austrian Fourth Army, had taken a prominent part in the just-concluded eastern offensive of the central powers (May to September, 1915), which proved to be successful but not decisive.
19. Cf. *Betrachtungen,* p. 28: "I have never been one of

those who would think . . . an easy and triumphal military victory for German . . . a piece of good fortune."

20. Cf. Thomas Mann's call for the foundation of a German academy, written in 1915 and reprinted in *Rede und Antwort,* pp. 291–295. At that time he thought of Munich as the seat of the academy, which was to comprise four groups for literature, music, the plastic arts, and "artistic life."

[7]

1. Presumably the proofs of Amann's article, *Leutnant Schimek in Memoriam;* cf. above, Letter 6 and Note 2.
2. Letter 6.

[9]

1. Amann's unpublished essay on Romain Rolland, which he had asked Thomas Mann to help him place; cf. Amann, *Politik und Moral,* p. 44, col. 2.
2. Sergei Dmitrievich Sasonov, 1860–1927, Russian Foreign Minister 1910–1916. His speech to the Duma, in which he called the war the greatest of crimes against humanity and placed the sole responsibility for it on Germany and her allies, was reprinted in extract in the *Frankfurter Zeitung* of February 23, 1916.
3. First the heading of an article by Romain Rolland in the *Journal de Genève* for September 15, 1914, then the title of the book, published in Paris in 1915 by Albin Michel, which contained various articles and essays of a humanitarian and pacifist character published by Rolland since the outbreak of the war. Cf. Notes 13 and 16 to Letter 1, and the body of that letter. In the present passage the book is meant; Thomas Mann had available the twenty-ninth edition of it (*Betrachtungen,* p. 140).

Notes

4. Rolland, *Au-dessus*, p. 30, where he calls *"Nécessité connaît pas de loi"* the Germans' Eleventh Commandment. Thomas Mann also condemns Rolland's translation of *"Not"* by *"nécessité"* in *Betrachtungen*, p. 151, where there are a good many echoes of this particular passage; cf. also *Betrachtungen*, p. 331. Incidentally, Amann appears to have agreed with Thomas Mann on this point; in any case, in a letter of Easter 1916 (cf. Note 9 to Introduction) he also charges Romain Rolland with having missed the deep resonance of the word *Not*.

5. An anticipation of the idea developed toward the end of this letter in opposition to Rolland's view of the intellectual.

6. These ideas concerning a better postwar Europe recur in more developed fashion, but with many verbal echoes, in the *Betrachtungen*, pp. 497–499, as "dreams dreamed on a pre-autumnal morn in 1917." Cf. Introduction, p. 16.

7. In *Politik und Moral* Amann speaks of underlinings, exclamation marks, and a "bravo" on the margin of his manuscript, "whose transfigured body still shines through my efforts at erasure."

8. *Die Weissen Blätter. Eine Monatsschrift.* Edited by Erik-Ernst Schwabach (later known as René Schickele), Leipzig.

9. Heinrich Mann's essay "Zola" appeared in Jahrgang 2, Heft 11 (November 1915), pp. 1312–1382.

10. Verbal echoes in *Betrachtungen*, p. 21, in the chapter "Der Zivilisationsliterat." Cf. Heinrich Mann's "Zola," *loc. cit.*, pp. 1363, 1368, and 1374.

11. Significantly, Thomas Mann mentions here only the covert attacks in the Zola essay upon imperial Germany, not those upon his own person. The first mention of this matter is to be found in Letter 27, apparently in response to a question of Amann's.

12. Since 1897 the *Neue Rundschau* had published many of Thomas Mann's writings. Even larger works like *Royal Highness* and *Death in Venice* first appeared here.

13. Presumably an ironic allusion to the appearance of his own war essays of 1914 and 1915 in the *Neue Rundschau*.

14. Paul Deschanel, 1855–1922, Left Republican, president of the French Chamber of Deputies 1898–1902 and 1912–1920. In *Gedanken* Thomas Mann refers to him as one of the most prominent of Germany's enemies (p. 30).

15. Gabriel Hanotaux, 1853–1944, politician and historian. Member of the French Academy.

16. Published 1912; the German translation by Jakob Hegner, which Thomas Mann had read, appeared in 1913. In *Betrachtungen,* pp. 404–406, Thomas Mann again speaks of the powerful impression this play made upon him. Here, too, he opposes the "true France," the *"douce France* of our dreams," to the France of the Allied politicians.

17. Letter 8.

18. Thomas Mann did not know the original passage, for it was not contained in the book edition to which he had access. He quoted the passage in Amann's translation from the latter's unprinted Rolland study, for which Amann was later to rebuke him; cf. Introduction, p. 18.

19. *Au-dessus,* pp. 146 f.

20. Goethe (Werke I, Bd. 2, p. 279 Sophien edition); cf. *Betrachtungen,* p. 517.

[10]

1. Amann's essay on Romain Rolland; see Letter 9.

2. "Exposure" in the technical sense, the term used in photographic parlance as equivalent to "lighting." Cf.

Thomas Mann's vexation with photographic proce-
dures: "In fact I prefer to sit for hours to a drafts-
man or a painter than to endure 'exposure' for two
hours; the process makes my nerves contract painfully." (*Pariser Rechenschaft,* 1926, p. 65.)
3. *The Magic Mountain,* pp. 52, 60, 70.
4. "Theodor Fontane und sein französisches Erbe," in
Euphorion, Bd. 21 (Jahrgang 1914), pp. 270–287,
623–653, 790–815.
5. "The Old Fontane" (in *Essays of Three Decades,* pp.
287–306) was first published in German in 1910.

[11]
Picture postcard. The colored picture shows the distribution of packages to German soldiers from a can-
vas-covered wagon. A wintry city, much destroyed.

[12]
1. Similarly in Letter 9; but the expression "civilization
literati" is used here for the first time.

[13]
1. April 23, 1916.
2. Letter 12.
3. "I am a mushroom that stays put; I do not travel without being driven to it." Schopenhauer to Adam Ludwig von Doss, in rejecting an invitation; letter of
January 19, 1855, in *Schopenhauer-Briefe,* ed. by
Ludwig Schemann, 1893, p. 276.
4. Equivalent to "Tsar's village"—former palace of the
Tsars in the vicinity of St. Petersburg.
5. Cf. the address *Lübeck als geistige Lebensform,* Lübeck,
1926, pp. 39 f.; also the idyll *Gesang vom Kindchen,*
where the wording is even closer to that of the letter
(p. 26 in the edition published at Munich 1919–
1920 by the Rupprecht Press).

6. The reference is probably to the essay "Das Theater als Tempel" in *Morgen. Wochenschrift für deutsche Kultur,* Jahrgang 1, 1907, pp. 214–217.
7. Jahrgang 32, Bd. 124 (1908), pp. 116–119, 259–290. The essay appeared as a contribution to a symposium on *The Cultural Values of the Theater.* Also in *Rede und Antwort,* 1922, pp. 18–66.
8. Similarly in Letter 12; also *Betrachtungen, "Vorrede,"* p. XII.
9. "Peoples and Fatherlands" is the title of the eighth section of *Beyond Good and Evil.* The following discussion of Nietzsche recurs in greater detail in the *Betrachtungen,* pp. 220 ff.
10. Allusion to Bismarck's remark at the session of the North German Reichstag of March 11, 1867: "Gentlemen, let us work swiftly! Let us put Germany into the saddle, so to speak! She will know how to ride." Similarly in *Betrachtungen,* p. 228: "A giant placed Germany in the saddle . . . "
11. Theodor Wolff, born 1868, died 1943 in the Sachsenhausen concentration camp; chief editor of the *Berliner Tageblatt* from 1906 on.
12. Thus, though without any direct reference to Wolff, almost in the same words in *Betrachtungen,* p. 473, in a passage presumably written in 1917.

[14]

1. Letter 12.

[15]

1. This is the first mention of the title. Where it was announced as an essay for the *Rundschau* is not clear.
2. Probably not Efraim Frisch, given as editor on the title page of the periodical, but Dr. August Mayer, *Privatdozent* at the University of Vienna, who is referred to in Letter 16 as editor of the *Neuer Mercur.*

Notes

[16]

1. The chapter "Einkehr" in the edition of 1918, pp. 31–67.
2. *Betrachtungen,* in the chapter "Gegen Recht und Wahrheit"; cf. Introduction, p. 17.
3. *Au-dessus,* pp. 25–26, Note, and pp. 120–142; cf. *Betrachtungen,* pp. 140 f. and p. 137, where these expressions are repeated in connection with the "debate" with Romain Rolland. One of the passages calls for special mention because it played a part in Amann's subsequent attack upon Thomas Mann in *Politik und Moral* (p. 46, col. 2). The passage was Rolland's charge that Thomas Mann wrote his comments on the war in 1914 *"dans un accès de délire d'orgueil et de fanatisme irrité."* In quoting this passage in *Betrachtungen,* pp. 141, 157, Thomas Mann omitted the possibly softening phrase *"accès de,"* for which Amann takes him to task.
4. See Note 2 to Letter 13.
5. The *Neue Merkur* published from 1914 to 1916 and then did not resume publication until 1919.
6. The "Polish Library," founded and edited by A. von Guttry and W. von Kościelski, was issued in several volumes between 1917 and 1919.
7. This suggestion that Amann publish a volume of his collected essays is taken up again later on (Letter 24).

[17]

1. Arthur Trebitsch, 1880–1927, a Viennese by birth, had attacked Thomas Mann's Frederick essay in his *Friedrich der Grosse. Ein offener Brief an Thomas Mann.* Trebitsch maintained that Thomas Mann had not done justice to the king's greatness; that he had distorted the whole personality by his "spiteful view of the pettiness and roguery of human nature." Great only in describing minutiae, Trebitsch said, he had

Notes

failed when he attempted to measure greatness with his customary yardstick.

2. Misunderstandings of this sort had occurred in more than one case, as is evident from the remark in *Betrachtungen*, p. 163, that the character study of the king, which "could affect simpler readers as a lampoon," had called forth "indignant retorts."

3. Thus Trebitsch, *loc. cit.*, pp. 36 f., directly after his sharp attacks upon the Frederick essay, speaks of Thomas Mann's "delightful novel of a confidence man" and of having had the "rare artistic pleasure" of hearing some parts of it from the author's own lips.

4. The comparison between the two novels recurs, in part in the same words, in *Betrachtungen*, p. 61; for the remarks on *Buddenbrooks* cf. also p. 53.

5. The reference is probably to the essay "Einkehr"—which was withheld from the January issue "for political reasons" (Letter 19) and appeared in the March, 1917, issue. This essay corresponded in essentials to the chapter by the same name in *Betrachtungen*, pp. 31–52. On the completion of this chapter by September, 1916, cf. above, Letter 16.

6. Titled "Der Taugenichts" in the *Neue Rundschau*, Jahrgang 1916, pp. 1478–1490. The essay, written for a new edition of Eichendorff's novella (H. V. Weber Verlag, 1914), was later included in *Betrachtungen* (especially pp. 372–379).

7. The December, 1916, issue of the *Neue Rundschau* contains no contribution by Thomas Mann.

[18]

1. Cf. Letter 17 and Note 5; also Letter 19.

2. It is not clear what the work here referred to, which was rejected by the *Frankfurter Zeitung* (cf. Letter 20), may have been. Probably not *Animal mirabile*, since

according to *Politik und Moral* that was not written
until Christmas, 1916.

3. Cf. Letter 17 and Note 6. On Amann's objections, cf.
Letter 19.

4. Similarly, *Betrachtungen,* p. 16.

5. Similarly, *Betrachtungen,* p. 15.

6. The following ideas (to the end of the paragraph) recur,
in several instances in the same words, in the *Betrachtungen,* pp. 184, 185, in a passage written
"after two years of war."

7. The reference is probably to the writer Emil Strauss,
honorary Doctor of the Philosophical Faculty of Freiburg im Breisgau. He, along with Thomas Mann, was
the subject of Amann's article in *Effort libre,* 1912;
cf. Letter 6 and Note 3.

[19]

1. Cf. Letter 17 and Letter 18.

2. The chapter "Bürgerlichkeit," *Betrachtungen,* pp. 68–
120, especially pp. 78 ff.

3. Cf. *Betrachtungen,* pp. 34 ff.

4. "Her [Ortrud in *Lohengrin*] essence is politics. A political man is repulsive, but a political woman is
frightful." (Wagner to Liszt, January 30, 1852.)
The passage is also cited in *Betrachtungen,* p. 90.

5. The reference is probably to the passage in *Ecce Homo*
in which Nietzsche refers to himself as the last antipolitical German.

6. As we know from *Politik und Moral,* p. 29, col. 2, the
matter in question was a reply to Amann's objection
in a letter that the Göttinger Seven, Uhland, and
Storm were political men too, after all. Thomas Mann
contested this objection in greater detail, with some
echoes of the present letter, in *Betrachtungen,* pp.
85 f. He did not succeed in convincing Amann, who
repeated his argument in the 1919 polemic.

Notes

7. The source of this quotation has not been established; it also appears in Thomas Mann's Carlyle essay in the *Frankfurter Zeitung* (see Note 8) and in *Betrachtungen,* pp. 245, 525. The idea appears in another form several times in Hegel's writings (Band 10, p. 440, Band 11, pp. 555, 564, in the Jubiläum edition).

8. In the feuilleton section of the *Frankfurter Zeitung* of December 24, 1916, entitled "Carlyles *Friedrich* in vollständiger deutscher Ausgabe." The subject of the review was the first of a planned six volumes of a new translation by Karl Linnebach of Carlyle's biography.

9. The article "Einkehr"; cf. above, Letter 17 and Note 5, also Letter 22.

10. The reference is to the article "Musik in München" in *Der Tag,* Berlin, No. 16/17, January 20/21, 1917.

11. Cf. above, Letter 6.

12. The German peace offer was made on December 12, 1916.

[20]

1. Cf. above, Letter 18 and Note 2.

2. *Animal mirabile,* also mentioned in *Politik und Moral,* p. 48, col. 2 (a "strange reverie, pensively written down at Christmas 1916, sixty-six hundred feet above sea level, amid avalanches, blizzards and displays of St. Elmo's fire") had according to a letter of Amann's (April 6, 1956) at first been intended as a Christmas amusement for the officers of his company, but then proved to be too serious. "Our group," Amann wrote, "was pictured as a herd of strange animals who had to carry out their foolish work of killing in 'our' terrain." Amann sent the manuscript to Romain Rolland at the time. Possibly it may be found in the archives of the Foundation Romain Rolland, Paris.

Notes

[22]
1. "To suffer with you . . ." Goethe, *Des Epimenides Erwachen,* Act 2, Scene 9. Also quoted in *Sketch,* p. 46.
2. The evacuation of the salient between Arras and Soissons and retreat to the so-called Siegfried Line, carried out between March 15 and 20, 1917.
3. The Revolution, which had broken out on March 18, 1917, and continued for a time, under Kerensky, to have a bourgeois character.
4. Gustave Hervé, 1871–1944, French journalist and politician, editor of the newspaper *La Victoire.*
5. In his speech of June 8, 1880, on the occasion of the unveiling of a monument to Pushkin, Dostoevsky attempted to reconcile the struggle between "Slavophiles" and "Westerners." He argued that the spirit of the Russian people contained an innate tendency to universality which constituted a mission, and that the Russians were destined to reconcile the contradictions of Europe and bring about a spiritual reunion of the nations of the Continent.
6. "Einkehr"; cf. Letters 17 and 19.
7. Cf. Letter 16.
8. The same thought also in the preface to *Betrachtungen,* p. ix, and in *Sketch,* p. 46.
9. Cf. Letter 4, where Thomas Mann referred to the interruption of his work on *The Magic Mountain.*
10. Giosuè Carducci, 1883–1907, Italian writer of political and anticlerical tendencies. In *The Magic Mountain,* pp. 58 ff., Settembrini is identified as a pupil of Carducci.
11. Concerning this expression, cf. Note 7 to Letter 4.
12. This justification for the wearisome and almost exclusively journalistic work on *Betrachtungen* remained vividly in Thomas Mann's mind even after completion of *The Magic Mountain.* As late as 1939 he still

referred to the "material unburdening" as a result of the "analytic-polemical work" without which the novel could not have become a work of art. (*Princeton*, p. 723.) Cf. similar remark in *Sketch*, p. 44, and see Introduction, p. 23.

13. The hundredth edition appeared in 1919.

14. The following remarks recur, in part in the same words, in *Betrachtungen*, pp. 200 f. Cf. also in the letter to Heinrich Mann of January 3, 1918 (in Kantorowicz, p. 113): "Thousands whom I helped to live."

15. The sentence "I did not pose . . . *Contrat social*" recurs almost in the same words in *Betrachtungen*, p. 199. Cf. also p. 385: "The Jacobin's operatic gesture, the expansive attitude in permanence—one hand on the heart, the other in the air"; also the above-mentioned letter to Heinrich Mann.

16. Allusion to Heinrich Mann's remarks in the Zola essay (*loc. cit.*, p. 1369), which Thomas Mann felt to be directed against himself.

17. Cf. Letter 17 on the contrast between *Buddenbrooks* and *Royal Highness*.

18. The Italians. Gabriele d'Annunzio was already mentioned in Letter 6.

[24]

1. According to Amann in a letter of May 1, 1956, an informal essay on an episode in the *Life of Benvenuto Cellini* (Book 2, Chapter 8): the dangerous crossing of Wallenstadt Lake. The article, "Benvenuto Cellini als Krieger," appeared as a feuilleton in the *Münchener Neueste Nachrichten* for May 3, 1917.

2. Cf. Letters 18 and 20.

3. The writer Dr. Kurt Martens, 1870–1945, mentioned by name in Letter 25. His acquaintanceship and friendship with Thomas Mann dated back to the beginning of the century; *Tonio Kröger* was dedicated

to him (incorrectly under the name of Karl Martens).
In 1917–1918 he performed what he called "patriotic auxiliary service" as features editor of the *Münchener Neueste Nachrichten.* Cf. Martens, *Schonungslose Lebenschonik,* Teil 2 (1924), pp. 26 f., 159–165; also *Sketch,* p. 20.

4. More concerning this plan in Letter 26.

[25]

1. Not in our collection.
2. In a letter of April 6, 1956, Amann informed us that he had been wounded on the Isonzo in the summer of 1917.
3. Cf. above, Note 3 to Letter 24. No printing of the *Animal* essay has been found in the *Münchener Neueste Nachrichten* for 1917–1918.
4. Thomas Mann did not in fact complete *Betrachtungen* until the end of 1917 (*Vorrede,* p. XI).
5. The date in the corresponding chapter of *Betrachtungen,* "At the end of the third year of the war" (p. 415), agrees with this statement.
6. The chapter "Einiges über Menschlichkeit" was written in the summer of 1917 (*Betrachtungen,* pp. 437, 499) and the chapter "Vom Glauben" in October, 1917 (p. 544).
7. The concluding two chapters planned here were combined into one ("Ironie und Radikalismus") in *Betrachtungen.*
8. The première of *Palestrina,* which opened a Pfitzner Week in Munich, took place on June 12, 1917, in the Prinzregenten Theater, Bruno Walter conducting.
9. The following sentences, down to "flimsy appearance," recur almost in the same words in *Betrachtungen,* pp. 407 f.
10. Quotation from Nietzsche, who applied these words to Richard Wagner: "I like in Wagner what I like in

Schopenhauer, the moral fervor, the Faustian flavor, the Cross, Death, and the Tomb." (Nietzsche to Erwin Rohde, October 8, 1868.) The passage is also quoted by Thomas Mann in his essay on Dürer in *Past Masters and Other Papers* (New York: Alfred A. Knopf, Inc., 1933), p. 151.

11. An allusion to Goethe's *Epilogue to Schiller's "Glocke,"* Str. 4 (*Werke* I, Bd. 16, p. 166, Sophien edition).

[26]

1. Probably for the publication of a collected edition of his printed and unprinted essays; cf. above, Letter 24. From the moment the question was raised Thomas Mann seems to have felt that any publication of this type could take place only after the war.

2. Korfiz Holm, 1872–1942, mentioned below by name. Thomas Mann attended *gymnasium* in Lübeck and later worked on *Simplizissimus* with him. Cf. *Sketch,* p. 16.

3. Oskar Bie, 1864–1938, writer on music, at that time editor of the *Neue Rundschau.*

[27]

1. One of the two mottoes on the title page of *Betrachtungen,* from *Les fourberies de Scapin* of Molière (II, 11). Similarly, in the letter of Heinrich Mann of January 3, 1918 (Kantorowicz, p. 113): "What lies behind me was a galley slave's work." Cf. Note 9 to Letter 5.

2. Letter 25.

3. Cf. *Betrachtungen,* p. 408: the work "is quite pertinent —pertinent to this book."

4. Entitled "Palestrine" in *Neue Rundschau,* Jahrgang 28, October, 1917, pp. 1388–1402. With minor additions, in *Betrachtungen,* pp. 407–428.

5. *Madame Legros,* published by Cassirer, Berlin, 1913;

première in 1917. The fate in this play of a French *petite bourgeoise* on the eve of the Revolution, who sacrifices her bourgeois existence to obtain the release of an innocent man from the Bastille, was also mentioned by Heinrich Mann in his Zola essay (*loc. cit.,* p. 1375) as a parallel to Zola's defense of Dreyfus.
6. Employing the same adjectives in *Betrachtungen,* p. 165, Thomas Mann demurs at naming whom he considers to be the spokesman for the "civilization literati."

[28]
1. According to *Betrachtungen,* p. xi, the last sections were written around the end of 1917.
2. Probably with reference to the Treaty of Brest-Litovsk, signed on March 3, 1918, which ended the war in the East on such favorable terms for Germany.
3. A possible explanation of this expression may be contained in *Betrachtungen,* p. 429, in which Thomas Mann speaks of the "three-part equation of classical Democratism: Reason equals Virtue equals Happiness." The expression recurs, along with other phrases from the letter, in *Betrachtungen,* p. xxxv.
4. This too—somewhat esoteric—this phrase also occurs in *Betrachtungen,* p. xxxv.
5. It is mentioned as imminent in a letter to Heinrich Mann of January 3, 1918 (in Kantorowicz, p. 110); Thomas Mann writes that he curses the necessity for such a trip, for which he is utterly disinclined at the moment.
6. Pfitzner was active in Strassburg from 1908 to 1918 as conductor and director of the Conservatory.
7. In *Sketch,* p. 46, Thomas Mann relates, with some rather biting humor, his visit in occupied Brussels, the production of *Fiorenza* by the German dramatic troupe, and a breakfast with General Hurt, the governor of the city.

Notes

8. Here Thomas Mann read (*Lübeckische Anzeigen* of January 19, 1918) in the Municipal Theater from his Schiller sketch, *A Weary Hour, Confessions of Felix Krull, Royal Highness,* and *The Infant Prodigy.*
9. Cf. Letter 10 and Note 4.
10. Conrad Wandrey, Ph.D., born 1887, author of *Theodor Fontane* (Munich, 1919), which was reviewed by Thomas Mann in the *Neuer Merkur* for July, 1921, and discussed in greater detail in *Rede und Antwort,* 1922, pp. 99–117. Wandrey, also the author of a monograph on Pfitzner (1922), later sharply criticized Thomas Mann's support of the Weimar Republic and Western democracy ("Thomas Mann und die 'Forderung des Tages'" in *Deutsche Rundschau* of March, 1930, Bd. 222, pp. 196–200).
11. Ernst Bertram, born 1884, poet and member of the Stefan George circle, later professor of literature in Cologne. His book, *Nietzsche. Versuche einer Mythologie,* was published in Berlin by Bondi, 1918. On his friendship with Thomas Mann, cf. *Sketch,* p. 47.
12. On Franz Ferdinand Baumgarten, see Letter 30 and Note 3.

[29]

1. No letter corresponding to this date is in our collection.
2. Probably *A Man and his Dog,* first published in 1919, written in 1918.

[30]

1. Elisabeth Mann, born in Munich in 1918. On the following, cf. *Sketch,* p. 33, and *Gesang vom Kindchen.*
2. This scene was not contained in the portion of *Felix Krull* published in 1922; as far as we know, it first appeared in the complete edition of *Felix Krull* published by Querido Verlag, Amsterdam, in 1948.
3. Franz Ferdinand Baumgarten, Ph.D., critic and novelist, died 1927. Author of *Das Werk Conrad Ferdinand*

Meyers. Renaissance-Empfinden und Stilkunst (Munich: Beck, 1917), mentioned in Letter 28 and discussed in more detail in *Betrachtungen,* p. 558.

4. The passage in Baumgarten (*loc. cit.,* p. 54 f.) reads: "Meyer was a *bourgeois manqué* and an artist with a guilty conscience. The prejudices of the bourgeois, which were in his blood, spoiled for him the freedom of the artist, and the temptations of his artistic blood weighed upon his bourgeois conscience."

5. This passage, obviously quoted from memory, from a letter of Stifter's to Joseph Türk of February 22, 1850 (reprinted in the edition of Stifter's letters by Johann Aprent, Bd. 1, 1869, p. 190) also turned up shortly before in a letter from Thomas Mann to his brother Heinrich, January 3, 1918, in that connection defending the political stand he had taken in the war (in Kantorowicz, p. 113). The passage is also quoted in *Betrachtungen,* p. 201, likewise in debate with Heinrich Mann.

6. *Betrachtungen,* published in 1918 by S. Fischer, Berlin, in one volume of xliv plus 611 pages.

[31]

1. Probably refers to *Tradition;* cf. Introduction, p. 8.
2. In *Politik und Moral.*
3. In *Sketch,* pp. 48–49, Thomas Mann writes somewhat differently of *Betrachtungen:* "I like indeed to think that the book has its meaning and value for the history of culture; not only the value of steadfastness, but in its character as a last great rear-guard action of the romantic middle-class mentality in the face of advancing 'modernity,' an action conducted not without gallantry."

[32]

1. Also in "Briefe an einen Schweizer" (*Altes und Neues,* 1953, p. 736): "I am receiving many letters. Strange

world, at bottom, in which a few simple words of truth should stir up such a sensation and so much gratitude. Are people so little accustomed to truth nowadays? Alas, that may well be the case. But one would be a wretch not to make use of the opportunity to fulfill the obligations of the writer's profession." The reference is no doubt to a letter from Thomas Mann to Dr. Edward Korrod, in which Thomas Mann publicly declared himself an "exile" writer. (*Neue Zürcher Zeitung* of February 3, 1936.)

2. The expatriation of Thomas Mann, and of his wife and his children, Golo, Monika, Elisabeth, and Michael, was made official by decree of the Ministry of the Interior of December 2, 1936, and published in the *Reichsanzeiger und Preussischer Staatsanzeiger* (official journal) of December 12, 1936. Cf. Klaus Mann, *The Turning Point,* New York: L. B. Fischer, 1942, pp. 272 ff.

3. The lecture was delivered on May 8, 1936, and published that same year by Bermann-Fischer in Vienna as *Freud und die Zukunft.* ("Freud and the Future," *Essays of Three Decades,* New York: Alfred A. Knopf, Inc., 1948.)

4. The first personal meeting between Thomas Mann and Amann took place, according to information from Frau Dora Amann, in 1937; cf. Introduction, p. 28.

[33]

1. The reference is to the third part of the *Joseph* novel, mentioned in Letter 32. The "phenomenon" on the jacket represents a sphinx.

2. Cf. at the end of this letter, "the good, the very good entertainment in violet and black." To what this refers is not known.

Notes

[34]

1. The reference is to *Joseph in Egypt;* cf. Letter 33.
2. *Tradition* had been suppressed in August, 1935.
3. Dr. Erich von Kahler, born 1885 in Prague, independent scholar and writer, left Germany in 1933 and since 1938 has lived in the United States. His book *Der deutsche Charakter in der Geschichte Europas* was published by Europa Verlag, Zürich, in 1937, and was reviewed by Golo Mann in *Mass und Wert,* Jahrgang 1 (1937/38), pp. 493–498. Cf. also Thomas Mann's essay on him in *Altes und Neues,* 1953, pp. 220–225.
4. Schocken Verlag, Berlin, founded in 1931 by Salmann Schocken, was among the Jewish publishing houses then permitted in Germany.
5. Franz Kafka's *Gesammelte Schriften,* planned in six volumes; volumes 1–4 were published in 1935 by Schocken Verlag.
6. Herbert Reichner, "Philobiblon" Verlag in Vienna; Paul Zsolnay Verlag in Vienna and Berlin.
7. Lion's book, *Thomas Mann in seiner Zeit,* was published by Max Niehans, Zürich, in 1935. On Lion, cf. Letter 35.
8. Hermann Hesse had favorably reviewed *Tradition* in the *Neue Rundschau,* Jahrgang 45, Bd. 2, pp. 745 f.
9. Gottfried Bermann, son-in-law of the Berlin publisher Samuel Fischer, who died in 1934. Bermann continued the publishing house in Vienna in 1936, and from 1938 on in Stockholm, under the name of Bermann-Fischer.
10. Carl von Ossietzky (1887–1938), leading German pacifist and until 1933 editor-in-chief of the *Weltbühne,* had at this time been transferred from imprisonment in concentration camp to a Berlin hospital. The Nobel Peace Prize for 1935 was conferred upon him on November 23, 1936. In 1935 Thomas Mann had

written an open letter to the Nobel Peace Prize com-
mittee, sharply satirizing the Hitler regime's alleged
love of peace and urging awarding of the prize to
Ossietzky. (Letter reprinted in *Carl von Ossietzky,*
by Felix Burger and Kurt Singer, Zürich, 1937, pp.
117–121; also in *Altes und Neues,* 1953, pp. 599–
603.)

11. The German mining engineer Stickling was condemned
to death in Novosibirsk on December 22, 1936, for
alleged participation in Trotzkyist agitation; the sentence was then commuted to a long prison term.

12. *The Beloved Returns.* Parts of this novel, whose first
German edition was published in 1939 by Bermann-
Fischer, Stockholm, appeared from 1937 to 1939 in
issues of the magazine *Mass und Wert.*

[35]

1. Frau Dora Amann has kindly informed us that this was
probably a trip of Amann's to Milan and Lake Como,
which he had to cut short because his wallet was
stolen by pickpockets.

2. In a letter Theodor Fontane wrote to his daughter Mete
on August 3, 1889; he was then in his seventieth
year. "All my plans are accompanied by the question:
'What is the good of it all?' A question that threatens
to take entire possession of me." The passage is also
cited by Thomas Mann in his essay "The Old Fontane" (*Essays of Three Decades,* p. 288).

3. The pending voyage to America is also mentioned in the
"Briefe an einen Schweizer" (*Altes und Neues,* 1953,
p. 740; letter of March 2, 1937). Here Thomas
Mann speaks of lectures to be given in the New
School for Social Research in New York.

4. Frau Dora Amann informs us that this was a utopia,
Pest im Paradise, which has not been published.

5. Ferdinand Lion, born 1883, biographer of Thomas

174

Mann (cf. Letter 34), edited the magazine *Mass und Wert* put out by Thomas Mann and Konrad Falke and distributed by Oprecht Verlag, Zürich.
6. Cf. Letter 34 and Note 12.

[36]

1. Presumably summer or autumn of 1937; in any case before September 13, 1937 (date of Letter 37), since here Amann's stay in Berg an der Drau is mentioned as past.
2. According to Letter 37, the manuscript consisted of French letters of World War I. As Amann informed us in a letter of April 6, 1956, a selection of such letters which had not reached their addressees were published by Claude Berry in the Parisian magazine *Europe* in 1932. Amann's translations of these "wonderfully expressive documents" were ultimately published in Prague in a short-lived German weekly.
3. He must, as Amann wrote us, have been connected with French military censorship of letters from the front.

[37]

1. Berg an der Drau, Carinthia.
2. The reference is presumably to the impending voyage to America mentioned in Letter 35.
3. Similarly in "Briefe an einen Schweizer," October 23, 1937 (*Altes und Neues*, 1953, p. 741): ". . . But now it is necessary to prepare lectures which I must give early next year in America. This time it is to be a huge tour, twelve or fourteen cities, deep into the West . . ."

[38]

1. "Sick visit" was Amann's term for a letter which he wrote upon hearing over the radio of Thomas Mann's accident.
2. *The Holy Sinner,* completion of which is reported in

Notes

Letter 40 of November 7, 1950. According to Jonas, *Fifty Years of Thomas Mann Studies*, 1955, this novel was first published (by S. Fischer) in 1951, while *Die Entstehung des Doktor Faustus* appeared in 1949 (Bermann-Fischer, Amsterdam).

3. In his letter Amann had spoken of a "class of veterans" at Mohawk College, Utica, New York, with whom he was reading Thomas Mann's novella *Tonio Kröger*. He enclosed translation samples by two of his students, one of whom was Goldberg, once of Berlin, who had taken part in the invasion.

[39]

1. The reference is to Romain Rolland's *Jean-Christophe;* Amann had said in his letter that he saw in it an interesting parallel to *Doktor Faustus* "purely in content, though certainly naïve and good-natured, almost rustic, compared with the sorrowful refinement of the German book."

2. In his letter Amann had referred to President Truman's victory over Thomas E. Dewey as a "sudden drop in temperature" which amounted to a "staying with existing mediocrity" and represented an "upsetting experience for us foreigners."

3. Refers to Amann's "psychological objection" to the portrayal of Adrian Leverkühn. Music and musicians especially, Amann argued, "cannot exist so utterly cold and remote from life" as this Faustus who "more and more becomes a Homunculus"—the homunculus of Goethe's *Faust,* that is.

4. Amann had given a description of the landscape around Lake Champlain in which he was living and where he had read *Doktor Faustus.*

5. "Kumpfish"—that is, in the manner of Professor of Theology Ehrenfried Kumpf (*Doktor Faustus,* Chapter XII), who spoke in a "picturesquely archaic style."

Notes

[40]

1. The copy of a letter with Amann's "belated birthday congratulations," dated October 28, 1950, is in the possession of the Municipal Library.

2. "The Years of my Life," *Harper's Magazine,* October, 1950.

3. Fritz Strich, born 1882, professor at the University of Berne, Switzerland, since 1929, author of several essays on Thomas Mann.

4. Carl Helbing, born 1897, Swiss historian and critic of literature, author of *Die Gestalt des Künstlers in der neueren Dichtung. Eine Studie über Thomas Mann* (Berne, 1922) and other essays on Thomas Mann.

5. Jean Rudolf de Salis, born 1901, since 1935 Professor of History at the Eidgenössische Technische Hochschule, Zürich. An extract from his speech, "Thomas Man zum 75. Geburtstag" was published in the *Neue Zürcher Zeitung* of June 9, 1950.

6. Hans Ewers, Member of the Bundestag and Senator ex officio, and Heinrich Marty brought congratulations to which several hundred signatures had been appended. An illustration of the marzipan cake (with the arms of the Mann family) appeared in the *Lübecker Nachrichten* of June 7, 1956.

7. Edmond Joachim Vermeil, born 1878, Professor of German Cultural History at the Sorbonne, 1934–1951.

8. Maurice Boucher, born 1885, professor at the Sorbonne since 1935. He is mentioned by Thomas Mann in "Pariser Rechenschaft," *The Dial,* January, 1927, p. 505, and with a description on pp. 506–507.

9. Jules Romains, born 1885, author, member of the Académie Française. He is mentioned in "Pariser Rechenschaft," pp. 94 f., "with his strong and plainly cut, affable face, that has a certain peasant quality." On his standing as creative writer, cf. *ibid.,* p. 95.

10. The thirty-eighth parallel, the border between South and

177

North Korea, was crossed on October 1, 1950, by
South Korean troops, and on October 9 by United
Nations troops under General MacArthur. Thomas
Mann means that as new citizens he and Amann
should not venture criticism of American policy—
and simultaneously makes a criticism by the image he
chooses.

[41]
Picture postcard of a landscape with palm trees and a
woman's figure in the right foreground.

[42]
Picture postcard showing a partial view of a room
with a desk on which stand a lamp, a framed photo-
graph, flowers, sculptures, candleholders, and writing
utensils. In front of the desk, a desk chair; in the
background of the room, pictures on the wall and a
grandfather clock.

1. We possess a copy of a letter of Amann's dated March
22, 1951.
2. "Otto Brechler in Memoriam (for January 9, 1951),"
later printed in Amann's collection of poems, *Kristall
meiner Zeit: Verschonte Verse 1914–1953*, Fairfield,
Connecticut, undated. Dr. Otto Brechler, Director of
the Manuscript Department of the Vienna National
Library, had been a friend of Amann's "in all the
realms of the arts and the intellect for forty-five
years." He died on January 9, 1951, at the age of
sixty-five. Cf. Introduction, p. 4.
3. *piano à queue:* grand piano

[43]
1. Presumably Frido, Michael Mann's son, the original of
little Echo in *Doktor Faustus*.
2. Presumably refers to a review by Friedrich Sieburg en-

titled "In der Sackgasse" ("In the Blind Alley"), which was published in *Gegenwart* of March 15, 1951, pp. 19 f.

3. *The Holy Sinner* (New York: Alfred A. Knopf, Inc., 1951), p. 91.
4. *Doktor Faustus,* Chapters XLIV and XLV.
5. Similarly in *Die Entstehung des Doktor Faustus,* 1949, p. 191.
6. Amann called Thomas Mann's attention to the review of *The Holy Sinner* published in the London *Times Literary Supplement* for April 27, 1951. At the same time Amman drafted a letter to the editor of the London *Times* protesting the viciousness of this review. We possess a copy of this letter, dated June 5, 1951; in the end Amann decided against sending the letter.
7. In his reply Amann informed Thomas Mann that he had misplaced the article.
8. Similarly, in 1953 Thomas Mann spoke of his "almost anxious wish to return home to the old soil in which I should like one day to rest." (*Nachlese,* 1956, p. 155; cf. also p. 192.)

[44]

1. Luther on January 19, 1536 (Kritische Gesamt-Ausgabe, Abteilung Briefwechsel, Band 7, p. 350).
2. As Professor Michael has kindly informed us, this paper has not yet been printed.
3. The passage in question, as Professor Michael has kindly told us, comes from *Die Geschichte vom braven Kasperl und dem schönen Annerl* in which the situation of a "writer by profession" is spoken of as somewhat suspect and embarrassing; the particular reference is the sentence: "One who lives by poetry has lost his balance, and an enlarged (i.e. overfed on one side) goose liver, no matter how good it may taste, always

presupposes a sick goose." (Brentano, *Werke,* ed. by
M. Preitz, Band 1, 1914, p. 353.)

4. This expression is not used in the above-mentioned
Brentano passage.

5. *New Research: Papers on the Intellectual History of the Germanic and Romance Peoples.*

6. Goethe to Eckermann on April 2, 1829.

7. Thus in the address *Germany and the Germans* (Library of Congress, 1945), p. 17.

8. Similarly, *Germany and the Germans,* p. 17.

9. Cf. Letter 34.

[45]

1. Thomas Mann's youngest son, Michael, born in 1919.

2. Yaltah Menuhin, sister of the famous violin virtuoso. The canceled concert is also mentioned in Amann's reply of November 18, 1951, of which we possess a copy.

3. Louise Seidler, 1786–1866, painter and writer. Her portrait of Riemer (oil painting) is in the reading room of the Thüringische Landesbibliothek in Weimar. There is a reproduction in the Pollmer edition of *Mitteilungen über Goethe.* The painting, as Arthur Pollmer writes in his introduction, shows Riemer "as a portly gentleman with a great deal of self-assurance."

4. In his reply of November 18, 1951, Amann contested this assumption on Thomas Mann's part: "I can very well recognize your Riemer in Louise Seidler's portrait. Here your instinct had already appropriated what it could use."

5. In Rome, where in 1802–1803 Riemer had stayed as a private tutor in the household of Wilhelm von Humboldt, Riemer had been seized by an unhappy passion for Caroline von Humboldt, the mother of his pupils. This incident is mentioned by Arthur Pollmer in the

introduction to his edition of Riemer's *Mitteilungen über Goethe.* Amann had called Thomas Mann's attention to this episode, "not bad as novel material," in his letter of October 28, 1950. In his reply to the present letter he referred to this "affair" again, remarking that Thomas Mann's having failed to notice it must be attributed to his creative unconscious which fended off disturbing even though interesting matter.

6. Cf. *The Beloved Returns,* New York: Alfred A. Knopf, Inc., 1940, p. 61.

7. The Riemer chapter first appeared in the magazine *Mass und Wert,* Nov./Dec. 1937. Concerning the attacks of infectious sciatica during which "the best chapters" of the book were written, see further in *Die Entstehung des Doktor Faustus,* 1949, p. 10.

[46]

1. Amann's letter of December 15, 1951.

2. Presumably from Letter 45. Amann had asked permission to quote these remarks. As far as we know, Amann's study of Riemer was not printed.

3. At the end of his letter of November 18, 1951, Amann had asked how the Krull story was developing.

4. In his letter of February 26, 1952, Amann spoke of this passage as showing Krull "involved in a spider's web of speculation on the nature of reality." He continued: "Actually, every swindler beats at this mysterious partition wall, and ultimately entangles himself in his own web."

[47]

1. The Accademia Nazionale dei Lincei had appointed Thomas Mann member of the Classe di Scienze morali, storiche e filologiche on October 5, 1947. In 1952 the International Literature Prize of the Feltrinelli Foundation, amounting to five million lire,

was awarded to him. His stay in Rome took place in the latter part of April, 1953. On April 29 he took part in a reception in his honor given by the Academy.

2. Amann replied to this letter on June 26, 1952; according to the copy, he discussed Thomas Mann's trip, illness, and the visits to Rome and Zürich.

[48]

Picture postcard showing the Fraumünster and the General Post Office in Zürich.

1. October 30, 1952, according to the copy.
2. Pacific Palisades, California.

NOTES TO THE DRAFT OF AMANN'S LETTER

1. *Gedanken.*
2. Amann was presumably thinking of two newspaper articles by Gerhart Hauptmann which were published in August and September, 1914: "Gegen Unwahrheit," and "Antwort an Herrn Romain Rolland." (For details see Viktor Ludwig, *Gerhart Hauptmann. Werke von ihm und über ihn,* 1931, p. 21.)
3. *Farcimentum;* cf. Letter 1 and Note 10.
4. Amann means Julius Robert Mayer, discoverer of the law of conservation of energy.
5. *Au-dessus.* Cf. Note 16 to Letter 1.
6. *Gedanken,* p. 1484. It is not quite clear how Amann's remarks apply to this passage.
7. Cf. Introduction, p. 18.
8. *Der Kanzler,* 1916, p. 127.
9. Amann means the American scholar Percival Lowell, whose book *The Soul of the Far East* appeared in German translation in 1911.
10. Jean de La Bruyère, 1645–1696, author of the *Caractères de Théophraste.*

11. Novel by Marie Madeleine Comtesse de La Fayette, 1634–1693.
12. François de Salignac de La Mothe-Fénelon, 1651–1715, Archbishop of Cambrai, author of *Les aventures de Télémaque.*
13. Jeanne Marie Bouvier de La Motte-Guyon, 1648–1717, French mystic.
14. Amann means Louis Reynaud, whose book was published by Hachette in 1914.
15. Hans von Kretschman, *Kriegsbriefe aus den Jahren 1870–71,* Berlin, 1903. The passages quoted are from the letters of November 18, 1870, and February 23, 1871.
16. Amann means Eyth's collection of letters, *Im Strom unsrer Zeit,* Gesammelte Schriften, Bd. 5, pp. 352, 354.
17. Similarly in *Der Kanzler,* 1915, p. 252.
18. Ferdinand Kürnberger, 1823–1879, Austrian writer.

Index of Persons

The figures refer to the correspondingly numbered letters of Thomas Mann; except that those marked "Ap." refer to the letter of Paul Amann printed in the Appendix, and those marked "Int." refer to the Introduction.

Index of Persons

Hanotaux, Gabriel, 9.
Hartmann von Aue, 38; 40; 42; 43.
Hauptmann, Gerhart, Ap.
Hegel, Georg Wilhelm Friedrich, 19.
Helbling, Carl, 40.
Hellman, 43.
Hervé, Gustave, 22.
Hesse, Hermann, 34; 40.
Hoffmann, E. T. A., 44.
Holm, Korfiz, 26 and Note 2.
Huch, Ricarda, Ap.
Hugo, Victor, 1; Ap.
Humboldt, Caroline von, née von Dacheröden, 45.
Jung-Stilling, Johann Heinrich, Ap.
Junker & Dünnhaupt (publisher), 44.
Kafka, Franz, 34.
Kahler, Erich von, 34.
Kant, Immanuel, 2.
Keller, Gottfried, 44; Int. p. 19.
Kretschman, Hans von, Ap.
Krupp (steel works), 28.
Kürnberger, Ferdinand, Ap.
La Bruyère, Jean de, Ap.
La Fayette, Marie Madeleine, Comtesse de, Ap. and Note 11.
Langen, Albert (publisher), 26.
Levetzow, Ulrike von, 5 and Note 6.
Lion, Ferdinand, 34–37.
Lowell, Percival, Ap.
Luther, Martin, 2; 27; 43; 44.
Mackensen, August von, 6.
Mann, Elisabeth, 30 and Note 1.
Mann, Frido, 43 and Note 1.
Mann, Heinrich, 9; 27; Int. p. 22.
Mann, Katja, née Pringsheim, 4; 21; 23; 30; 43.
Mann, Klaus, 4.
Mann, Michael, 45.
Mann, Thomas, writings of:
    Bekenntnisse des Hochstaplers Felix Krull (Confessions of Felix Krull, Confidence Man), 4; 17; 30; 42; 46.

187

Index of Persons

Betrachtungen eines Unpolitischen (*Reflections of a Non-Political Man*), 8; 9; 12; 13; 15–17; 19; 22; 25; 27; 28–31; Int. pp. 13–24.

Brief an die Zeitung "Svenska Dagbladet," Stockholm (*Letter to the Stockholm Newspaper "Svenska Dagbladet"*), 4; Int. pp. 12, 16.

"Ein Brief an Dr. Eduard Korrodi" ("Letter to the Dean of the Philosophical Faculty of the University of Bonn"), 32 and Note 1.

Buddenbrooks, 4; 6; 17; 22.

"Carlyles Friedrich in vollständiger deutscher Ausgabe" ("Carlyle's *Frederick* in a Definitive German Edition"), 19.

Doktor Faustus, 38–40; 43; Int. p. 28.

"Einkehr" ("Introspection"), 17; 19; 22 and Note 6.

"Die Entstehung des Doktor Faustus" ("The Making of *Doctor Faustus*"), 38; 39.

Der Erwählte (*The Holy Sinner*), 38 and Note 2; 40; 42; 43.

Fiorenza, 28.

"Freud und die Zukunft" ("Freud and the Future"), 32 and Note 3.

Friedrich und die grosse Koalition (*Frederick and the Great Coalition*), 1; 2; 12; 14; 17 and Note 1; Ap.; Int. pp. 13, 16.

"Gedanken im Kriege" ("Thoughts in War"), 1 and Note 3; Ap. and Note 1; Int. pp. 12, 14, 18, 20.

"Gedanken zum Kriege" ("Thoughts on the War"), 4 and Note 15.

Joseph und seine Brüder (*Joseph and his Brothers*), 32; 33 and Note 1; 34; Int. p. 26.

Königliche Hoheit (*Royal Highness*), 6; 17; 22; 26.

Lotte in Weimar (*The Beloved Returns*), 34 and Note 12; 35; 45; Int. p. 28.

"Meine Zeit" ("The Years of My Life"), 40 and Note 2.

"Musik in München" ("Music in Munich"), 19 and Note 10.

"Palestrina," 27 and Note 4.